Principles of Applied Behavior Analysis for Behavior Technicians (BTs) and Other Practitioners

Michele D. Wallace
G. Roy Mayer
California State University, Los Angeles

2017
Sloan Publishing
Cornwall on Hudson, NY 12520

Library of Congress Cataloging-in-Publication Data

Names: Wallace, Michele, 1968- author. | Mayer, G. Roy, 1940- author.
Title: Principles of applied behavior analysis for behavior technicians and other practitioners / Michele Wallace, G. Roy Mayer, California State University, Los Angeles.
Description: Cornwall on Hudson, NY : Sloan Publishing LLC, [2017]
Identifiers: LCCN 2017006887 | ISBN 9781597380676
Subjects: LCSH: Behaviorism (Psychology)
Classification: LCC BF199 .W24 2017 | DDC 150.19/43--dc23
LC record available at https://lccn.loc.gov/2017006887

Cover photo: © Bialasiewicz | Dreamstime.com - <a href="https://www.dreamstime.com/stock-photo-having-fun-child-therapy-session-shot-smiling-little-boy-sitting-white-chair-holding-his-teddy-bear-talking-image73613059#res11125791-">Having Fun At A Child Therapy Session Photo</a>

© 2017 by Sloan Publishing, LLC

Sloan Publishing, LLC
220 Maple Road
Cornwall-on-Hudson, NY 12520

All rights reserved. No portion of this book may be reproduced, in any form or by any means, without permission in writing from the Publisher.

Printed in the United States of America

ISBN-10: 1-59738-067-9
ISBN-13: 978-1-59738-067-6

Contents

Preface   v

1. An Introduction to Applied Behavior Analysis   1
2. Practicing Ethically   8
3. Introduction to Behavior Analysis Principles and Terms   17
4. Measuring Behavior   32
5. Reporting Behavioral Data   42
6. ABCs of Assessment   60
7. Skill Acquisition   75
8. Antecedent Procedures in Skill Acquisition   93
9. Generalization and Maintenance   104
10. Preventing Problem Behavior Through Introducing and Modifying Antecedents   117
11. Extinction and Differential Reinforcement Procedures to Reduce Problem Behavior   131
12. Punishment and Crisis Management   146
13. Comprehensive Behavior Planning   164

References   175

Preface

With the increase in the number of children diagnosed with autism and the push for evidence-based treatment for various conditions, it is no wonder we have seen an increase in the need for applied behavior analysis services. With this explosion in need has also come a demand for competent behavior analysis service providers at multiple levels: behavior technicians as well as behavior analysts. The profession of providing these services has become well defined, thanks to the Behavior Analysis Certification Board. They have developed various levels of certification professionals, the most recent being the Registered Behavior Technician (RBT). Although behavior technicians and other paraprofessionals have been implementing applied behavior analysis programs for decades, it is with this new development that as a field we have to address what knowledge and competencies these service providers should have. Having written another text geared towards more advanced levels of behavior analyst training, *Behavior Analysis for Lasting Change, Third Edition* (Mayer, Sulzer-Azaroff, & Wallace, 2014), we recognized the need for a text that explains applied behavior analysis and trains behavior technicians and other practitioners to be able to implement behavior services with competency and confidence, and thus was the birth of the idea for this text.

Our goals in this text were to explain applied behavior analysis in less technical terms, to give the reader a flavor for what they would be learning and doing as a behavior service provider. In addition, we wanted to ensure the basic principles were covered, and how to apply this knowledge within professional settings (day programs, community settings, classrooms, and homes) where the individual would be charged with changing behavior in meaningful ways. Finally, within a behavior analytic approach to training, we wanted to give the student the tools for meeting the behavioral competencies set out by the profession for the basic skills necessary to be an effective service provider. We hope to have accomplished these goals within this 13-chapter text that includes goals and objectives, content knowledge and chapter-ending Exercise and Activity sections geared toward ensuring behavioral competency of specific skills. However, as only true behavior analytic practice would dictate, we won't know if we have reached our goals until the data comes in.

It is our hope that the pages of this book will be read with notes written in the margin over and over again. In addition, we hope that this book will become your go-to resource when faced with questions or challenges while providing behavioral services. The Goals, Exercises, and Activities sections were provided with the hope that students will do them over and over again until they are confident they can competently implement the tasks required of a RBT. The exercises and activities should provide great material for the supervisor to discuss with the future RBT. Sample answers are available for instructors in a special section on the book's website (www.sloanpublishing.com/rbt).

Acknowledgements

This text started out as a need, turned into an idea, but was brought to fruition because of the dedication of many who have contributed to this text in multiple ways. Many of the examples and ideas for explaining topics have come from the thousand of interactions the authors have had with students as well as practicing professionals. We are especially thankful for Lucy Ainsman, graduate student at SDSU and employee of the Encinitas Union School District, and Sabrina Colombeau, BCBA at Gateway Learning Group, Delores Fraser McFadden, RBT supervisor and Adjunct Professor at Orange County (NY) Community College, Janet Burke of the Western Connecticut State University, and Jen Porter of George Brown College, who reviewed and provided editorial comments and suggestions for various parts of the text.

It goes without saying that this idea would have remained just an idea if it weren't for our fabulous editor, Bill Webber. From the inception of the text through its final publication, Bill has provided us with opportunity, support, flexibility, and marketing.

Each of us has personally sacrificed to make this dream come true, and we would not have been able to do this without our friends and family. Michele thanks her children (Payton and Aiden) for their understanding when mommy had to write and for the numerous examples of the application and success of behavior analytic practices at home. She would also like to thank friends and family who have continuously encouraged her along the way. She also extends a great deal of appreciation for her long time-mentor, Dr. Brian Iwata, for without his guidance and insight this would not have even been an idea.

Roy thanks his family (wife, mother, sister, two children, and seven grandchildren) for their support and understanding. He gives special thanks to Beth Sulzer-Azaroff for the support and enlightenment she has provided throughout his professional career. A special thanks also goes to Michele for getting him involved in helping to write this text. It turned out to be a fun, rewarding experience.

About the Authors

Michele D. Wallace Ph.D., BCBA-D is a full time professor at California State University, Los Angeles and is the program director for the Applied Behavior Analysis Program. Dr. Michele Wallace graduated from the University of Florida in 2000 with her doctorate in the Experimental Analysis of Behavior under the guidance of Dr. Brian Iwata. Dr. Wallace is on the Board of Editors for the Journal of Applied Behavior Analysis and has served as a guest reviewer for many other behavioral journals. She has been a Board Certified Behavior Analyst in the State of Florida since 1993 and a National Board Certified Behavior Analyst since 2000. Dr. Wallace has served on various professional boards including the Nevada Association for Behavior Analysis, California Association for Behavior Analysis, and the Behavior Analysis Certification Board. In addition, she has served as a behavior consultant to many agencies and school districts all over the United States and in China and Taiwan. She has authored and co-authored books, chapters, articles, and numerous presentations. Dr. Wallace is also the co-owner of BrainFIT, which is a behavior agency providing academic coaching to children. Finally, she is the proud behavioral mom of two amazing children (Payton and Aiden).

G. Roy Mayer, Ed.D., BCBA-D is Professor Emeritus at California State University, Los Angeles. He obtained his doctorate at Indiana University in 1966, taught at Southern Illinois University for 3 years, and then at CSULA for about 30 years. In 2008, he also served as Visiting Professor at NamSeoul University, South Korea. Dr. Mayer is one of the co-founders of Cal-ABA, served as its Program Co-Chairman and President, and received recognition from Cal-ABA as an Outstanding Contributor to Behavior Analysis. He also was recognized with the Outstanding Professor Award from CSULA. He has served on various editorial boards, has published numerous behavioral articles, and published a number of chapters and books (including one book that was translated into Korean and another into Spanish). He has given over 100 presentations, including several keynote addresses, has served as consultant to various school districts, and supervised in-home RBTs. He also has a life-time California Service Credentials in counseling, school psychology, social work, and child welfare and attendance. Currently, he teaches ABA part-time at San Diego State University, enjoys teaching others about ABA through his writing and teaching, and enjoys his family and the San Diego weather.

Chapter 1

Introduction to Applied Behavior Analysis (ABA)

GOALS

1. Define Applied Behavior Analysis.
2. Describe the seven dimensions of Applied Behavior Analysis.
3. Explain the role of the Behavior Analysis Certificate Board.
4. Describe the various certificate levels (RBT, BCaBA, BCBA, and BCBA-D).
5. Describe the requirements to become an RBT.
6. Describe the role of an RBT in comparison to the other certificate levels.
7. Describe the categories of the code of professional and ethical behavior of behavior analysts.
8. Complete this chapter's Exercises and Activities or those assigned by your instructor

Applied Behavior Analysis (ABA) is the area of behavior analysis which focuses on the application of procedures derived from the principles of behavior analysis to influence socially important behavior. ABA is based upon the scientific foundation of the Experimental Analysis of Behavior and the philosophy of Behaviorism. Generally speaking, ABA is characterized as focusing on factors such as *behavior*, utilizing behavioral principles, emphasizing identifiable variables within the environment, utilizing detailed procedures in systematic ways, and emphasizing the demonstration of behavior change via objective measurement. Moreover, ABA focuses on environmental (as opposed to mentalistic) explanations of the causes of behavior. *What does this all mean?* Basically, ABA focuses on what people say or do and changes in a person's behavior. It is mainly concerned with implementing specific procedures to change the environment to produce measurable and lasting behavior change. All subjective *assumptions* (descriptions of behavior such as "sad" or "mean") are removed from the equation and replaced with objective facts (actions such as crying or hitting).

For example, if I am trying to lose weight and I break my diet, an ABA approach would assess my environment (e.g., is there junk food in my pantry?) and implement a specific procedure (e.g., removal of all junk food from the house), and objectively measure progress (e.g., calories consumed, minutes spent working out, and weight) to determine the success of the intervention. Moreover, I would remind myself not to say, "I cannot lose weight, because I have low self-esteem."

It would be an injustice to introduce you to ABA without briefly discussing the seven dimensions that have really shaped the field. Baer, Wolf, and Risely (1968) proposed seven dimensions to guide the field and practice of ABA:

1. *Applied*—focuses on socially significant behaviors
2. *Behavioral*—focuses on objective measurement (what the behavior looks like)
3. *Analytic*—demonstrates functional relationships
4. *Technological*—fully describes all procedures implemented in such detail that someone could replicate implementation

5. *Conceptually Systematic*—utilizes procedures based upon principles of behavior analysis
6. *Effective*—demonstrates behavior change through objective measurement
7. *Generality*—behavior change that is produced across behaviors, people, and settings.

Practitioners of behavior analysis provide services within these seven dimensions of ABA. In other words, practitioners utilize these seven dimensions to guide their work. They are sure to choose socially significant behaviors, or behaviors that will change the client's future in significant ways, and focus on behavior that is measurable (either what the person says or does). It is important to demonstrate that the intervention they implement is responsible for behavior change, and not some other variable. They must provide a step-by-step description of all interventions implemented so that others can continue to implement the procedure. Practitioners ensure that the interventions they implement are based upon the principles of behavior analysis, are evidence-based, and establish that a measurable change in behavior is observed. Behavior analysts ensure change across more than one environment (home and school), people (mom and dad), or behaviors (aggression and tantrums). *So, how can you ensure you are following these dimensions as a practitioner?* First and foremost, it is important to understand in more detail what these dimensions mean. These dimensions are expanded upon throughout this book. You will learn how to choose, define, and measure behavior to help meet these dimensions of ABA: *applied*, *behavioral*, and *effective*. Its procedures are based upon the principles of behavior analysis to help meet the *technological*, *conceptually systematic*, *effective*, and *generality* dimensions, and they illustrate how to evaluate outcomes to help you meet the *analytic* and *effective* dimensions.

Before we embark on this journey, you may be wondering if there is a body that oversees the practice of ABA, and how you go about becoming a practitioner. Let's spend some time discussing the body that oversees the credentialing of practitioners and the practice of ABA.

THE BEHAVIOR ANALYSIS CERTIFICATION BOARD (BACB) AND CERTIFICATION

The Behavior Analysis Certification Board is a nonprofit corporation that oversees the professional credentialing needs related to behavior analysis services. The mission of the BACB is to protect consumers of behavior analysis by establishing, promoting, and disseminating professional standards. Moreover, their global vision is to increase the availability of qualified behavior analysts. The BACB website provides information regarding what behavior analysis is, requirements for credentialing at the different levels, ethical and practice guidelines, information regarding how to apply and sit for the exam, task lists regarding areas of knowledge in the field, information on continuing education, certificate registry, approved course sequences to qualify for the exam, how to maintain credentials, newsletters, and how to report a disciplinary action.

There are four levels of certification: Board Certified Behavior Analyst – Doctoral (BCBA-D), for individuals with doctoral training in behavior analysis; Board Certified Behavior Analyst (BCBA), for those with graduate-level education; Board Certified Assistant Behavior Analyst (BCaBA), for those with an undergraduate level of education; and Registered Behavior Technician (RBT), for those with a high school or higher level of education.

BCBA-Ds and BCBAs are independent practitioners who provide behavior-analytic services and can supervise the work of BCaBAs and RBTs. BCaBAs may not practice independently and must be supervised by either a BCBA-D or a BCBA. They may supervise RBTs under the supervision of a BCBA-D or BCBA. An RBT is a paraprofessional who may only practice under the direct supervision of a BCBA-D, BCBA, or a BCaBA. Generally, BCBA-Ds and BCBAs design assessment plans and interventions, while BCaBAs and RBTs implement these plans. BCaBAs and RBTs are considered the front-line staff and are the ones who directly work with clients on a routine basis, while the other practitioners oversee the program in a consultative format. *One could say that the RBTs are the ones who directly change behavior*. What an amazing profession, to be the one responsible for changing people's behavior in socially significant ways to better their lives and the lives of those around them. *So you may be wondering (and we hope you are), how do I become an RBT?* Lets look at the requirements necessary to become an RBT or behavior change agent.

RBT REQUIREMENTS

RBTs must be at least 18 years of age, have a high school diploma (or equivalent), complete 40 hours of training related to behavior analysis by a certified provider, complete a criminal background check, complete and pass the *RBT Competency Assessment*, and pass the *RBT Examination*. Moreover, RBTs are required to complete and pass the *RBT Competency Assessment* annually. Every RBT must have a certificant (BCBA-D, BCBA, or BCaBA) who is responsible for ensuring the RBTs is obtaining ongoing supervision for a minimum of five percent of the hours they are providing behavior-analytic services per month. The supervision must include at least two face-to-face, synchronous contacts per month during which the supervisor observes and provides feedback regarding the RBT service delivery. In addition, at least one of the two contacts must be one-on-one[1].

If you are at least 18 years of age, have a high school diploma or equivalent and you want to be a RBT, the first step in becoming an RBT is to find an approved 40-hour training. There are a number of on-line providers that provide this 40-hour training and can be found by doing a search of the web using the terms "RBT training." In addition, there are university-based programs that will allow you to take an RBT course that counts for this training requirement as well as a course toward your college degree. Once you have completed this training, passed your assessment, or are still in the process of completing this training, you will need to secure a "responsible certificant" (a BCBA-D, BCBA, or BCaBA) who agrees to be responsible for your RBT supervision. This is generally achieved by finding a behavioral agency and either securing employment or an internship.

One important aspect of becoming an RBT is to understand the ethical parameters guiding the practice of behavior analysis. One can

---

[1]These requirements are based upon the standards presented by the BACB in January 2016 and are subject to change. Please review the BACB website for the most current requirements.

obtain the contents of the *Professional and Ethical Compliance Code for Behavior Analysts* (PECC) from the BACB website (bacb.com). The ethical standards of practice are just as important to know as the principles of behavior analysis. The PECC is related to the professional and ethical behavior of behavior analysts regardless of their certificant level. The PECC is comprised of 10 sections including: Responsible Conduct of Behavior Analysts; Behavior Analysts' Responsibility to Clients; Assessing Behavior; Behavior Analysts and the Behavior-Change Program; Behavior Analysts as Supervisors; Behavior Analysts' Ethical Responsibility to the Profession of Behavior Analysis; Behavior Analysts' Ethical Responsibility to Colleagues; Public Statements; and Behavior Analysts Research.[2] Although specifically addressing all the nuances of the PECC is beyond the scope of this text, all RBTs should become familiar with and follow this code prior to practicing behavior analysis. Thus, the next chapter provides a summary of the PECC and the responsibility of an RBT. With that said, it is important to point out that depending on where you are working as an RBT, and in what country or state, there are other ethical codes and laws that govern the work that you do. Thus, besides understanding the PECC, it is important to look into the ethics and professional laws that pertain to the work you will be doing. For example, if you will be an RBT in a school setting, then state and local educational laws will also affect how you perform your job.

SUMMARY AND CONCLUSIONS

A layperson's definition of applied behavior analysis would be the use of interventions that have proven to be effective to alter important behavior across situations. The practice of ABA is based upon seven dimensions including: applied, behavioral, analytic, technological, conceptually systematic, effective, and generality. The board that oversees the practice of ABA by RBTs, BCaBAs, BCBAs, and BCBA-Ds is the BACB. The board provides requirements, scope of practice, and professional and ethical codes of conduct for behavior analysts at all levels. Professional and Ethical conduct is as important in practic-

---

[2]Based upon the published code on the BACB website January 2016.

ing behavior analysis as understanding the concepts, procedures, and principles of behavior analysis.

EXERCISES

After you have completed the exercises below, you will want feedback. Your instructor has access (or can obtain access from the publisher) to sample answers for each of the following exercises:

1. List what your supervision (as an RBT) must include.
2. Specify what behavior is.
3. What is an important distinction that separates ABA from other disciplines?

ACTIVITIES

1. Describe yourself and your experiences in ABA.
2. Why have you decided to participate in this experience? What do you hope to gain from it?
3. Identify the long-term goals, vision, and/or purpose of your host organization and how your participation can contribute toward them.
4. Go to the Behavior Analysis Certification Board's website (www.bacb.com) and
    a. Specify a definition of behavior analysis.
    b. Specify the requirements for becoming a registered behavior technician (RBT)
    c. Print out the RBT task list that specifies what you need to know to sit for the *RBT Competency Assessment* and examination
5. Review the *Professional and Ethical Compliance Code for Behavior Analysis* (PECC) (bacb.com/ethics-code/).

Chapter 2

Practicing Ethically

GOALS

1. Define ethics.
2. Describe what it means to practice ethically.
3. Describe briefly the 10 sections of the code.
4. Describe the role that evidence-based practices play in ABA.
5. Specify the code that requires behavior analysts to stay abreast of the current research and practice of the field.
6. Specify what the behavior analyst's top priority is when delivering services.
7. Identify what must occur before implementing treatment.
8. Describe what truthful and untruthful reporting includes.
9. List what must occur before you can call yourself an RBT or Behavior Analyst.
10. Complete this chapter's Exercises and Activities or those assigned by your instructor.

If you are like us, you know that you should behave ethically, but you might not be able to describe exactly what that means. Thus, it might be useful first to understand what ethics means and then go over some specifics with respect to practicing ethically as an RBT.

Ethics is actually a branch of philosophy that involves identifying and recommending concepts of right and wrong (or good vs. evil, virtue vs. vice) actions. In general, this branch of philosophy is geared toward answering the questions: "what is the best way for people to live?" and "what behaviors are right or wrong in certain situations?" Given that ABA influences the behavior of our fellow humans, it is important that such an application of services be provided in an ethical manner. As such, one important aspect of becoming an RBT is to understand the ethical parameters guiding the practice of behavior analysis. Practicing ethically means following the ethical and professional guidelines set out by the profession. Because ethical views vary from person to person, especially when working with diverse populations, concrete ethical guidelines help practitioners define and justify expected and unexpected ethical behavior (e. g. 'best practice') in complicated situations where the boundary is not as clear. One can obtain the contents of the Professional and Ethical Compliance Code for Behavior Analysts (PECC) from the BACB website (bacb.com). It is imperative to point out, that knowing the ethical standards of practice are just as important as knowing the principles of behavior analysis.

As stated in the previous chapter, the PECC is comprised of 10 sections related to professional and ethical behavior of behavior analysts regardless of certificate level including: Responsible Conduct of Behavior Analysts, Behavior Analysts' Responsibility to Clients, Assessing Behavior, Behavior Analysts and the Behavior-Change Program, Behavior Analysts as Supervisors, Behavior Analysts' Ethical Responsibility to the Profession of Behavior Analysis, Behavior Analysts' Ethical Responsibility to Colleagues, Public Statements, Behavior Analysts Research, and Behavior Analysts' Ethical Responsibility to the BACB. Although specifically addressing all the rights and wrongs of practicing ABA is beyond the scope of this text, all RBTs should become familiar with and follow this code prior to practicing behavior analysis. Lets take a cursory look at the PECC codes that pertain to practicing as an RBT.

Responsible Conduct of Behavior Analysts (Code 1.0)

RBTs must "maintain the high standards of behavior of the profession (BACB, 2016)." This is achieved by *behaving* according to these standards (remember, behavior is what people do and say). One of these standards include relying on evidence-based knowledge (i.e., knowledge based upon systematic research) when making scientific or professional judgments (service delivery). Thus, it is unacceptable to implement non-evidence-based interventions. Although related fields may conduct interventions based on their theories and practices, unless these strategies are evidence-based practices, RBTs may not implement these other strategies. For example, because the use of vitamins is *not* an evidence-based practice in improving behavior problems in children diagnosed with autism, it would not be appropriate for an RBT to suggest or implement such a strategy with a client. This is an important distinction that separates behavior analysis from other disciplines. *Before a procedure is implemented with a client, it must have empirical evidence to support its use.*

In addition, behavior analysts should only practice within the boundaries of their competence based upon education, training, and supervision experience. If they want to provide services, teach, or conduct research outside of their area of competence, they must obtain appropriate experience and training in those areas. Thus, if you have never been trained on how to implement a feeding program, you should not be implementing one. Moreover, behavior analysts commit to maintaining competence through professional development and stay abreast of the current research literature. Yes, this means you need to read articles, attend conferences and workshops, and seek out training opportunities. If your supervisor asks you to conduct a procedure for which you have not been trained, you must speak up and inform him or her that you need training before you can implement that procedure.

Another standard of the profession is to provide services with integrity, which means being truthful and conforming to legal and ethical codes. Remember, being truthful does not mean turning a blind eye to untruthful practices. If the behavior analyst you are working under asks you to do something that is unethical or untruthful, you should not do it. Furthermore, you have an obligation to report their unethical behavior to the BACB.

This code also explains that RBTs only provide services within a professional role and are both socially and culturally aware. Thus, a friend who asks you for help with their child during happy hour would not constitute a professional relationship. You should *not* provide services to your friend or her child. Moreover, make sure you understand cultural diversity prior to working with an individual. Cultural practices can influence how procedures are implemented and whether a specific procedure is acceptable.

Regarding client-technician relationships, behavior analysts avoid dual relationships (e.g., friend and technician). One guideline that prevents multiple relationships from forming includes not accepting gifts or giving gifts to clients. Similarly, behavior analysts do not exploit persons whom they have actual or perceived power over, including refraining from sexual relationships with clients, students, or supervisees. As an RBT you will be spending a lot of time with a family and a specific professional. It is easy to see how these lines can become blurry if you do not toe the line. For example, the parents of your client might start to think of you as part of the family because you spend more time with them than their extended family. So, of course they want to buy you a birthday present. It is important to have the conversation about avoiding dual relationships with them upfront, rather than risk hurting their feelings later on. Let them know you understand that you will become close because of all the time you will be spending with their family, but it is extremely important for everyone to keep the relationship professional.

Behavior Analyst Responsibilities to Clients (Code 2.0)

RBTs have a responsibility to all parties affected by the delivery of services. For example, they have a responsibility to the student, the teacher, the principal, parents, other students, etc. when providing services in a school. However, their top priority is to advocate for the best interest of the individuals whose behaviors are being changed. This is hard for some professionals to understand. As an RBT, your primary concern is the best interest of your client. In fact, the rights of your clients are paramount.

It is the responsibility of the behavior analyst to obtain permission to electronically record service delivery prior to recording. However, documentation and recording of objective data are essential when providing behavior analytic services, and they must be consistent with best practice and the law. If you are providing services in a school, you must have permission from all the students' parents in the class before recording. Even if you think the parents will like that you're recording when your client had such a great day, do *not* record under any circumstances without consent to record. In addition, records should be kept in a secure location for seven years.

Given that you will be a representative of the profession as an RBT, you should be able to inform clients where they can lodge professional complaints. Moreover, RBTs must comply with criminal background checks and provide valid documentation.

In providing services, RBTs ensure confidentiality and only discuss the case within a professional role (do *not* post information on social media, and no selfies with clients). Moreover, RBTs do not disclose confidential information (including the client's name, age, disability, assessment results and more) without the consent of the client or as mandated by law. Unless you have explicit consent to discuss the case, you should not be talking about the case, this includes friends, spouses, etc. RBTs also are mandated reporters of abuse.

Assessing Behavior (Code 3.0)

The first step in any behavior change program is assessment. Thus, prior to developing and implementing behavior change interventions, an appropriate assessment must be completed. Moreover, the results of these assessments must be in the convention of behavior analytic practices and utilized for making decisions (visual inspection). In other words, when you are working with a client, the results of these assessments will be the foundations for creating and implementing interventions and must be presented in written form. Thus, as an RBT you must ensure an appropriate assessment was conducted prior to your implementing any behavior intervention plan. This can be accomplished by asking to see the assessment results when you first get put on a case.

Behavior Analysts' Ethical Responsibility to the Profession of Behavior Analysis (Code 6.0)

Regardless of other professional training (educator, social worker, etc.), RBTs uphold and advance the values, ethics, and principles of the profession of behavior analysis. In addition, you have an obligation to the profession to participate in professional or scientific organizations or activities. Thus, it is important that you attend conferences, workshops, and in-services. Moreover, you must make sure that you are promoting behavior analysis by making information regarding behavior analysis available to your clients and the public. Make sure you have access to resources on behavior analysis to give to those who need them.

Behavior Analysts' Ethical Responsibility to Colleagues (Code 7.0)

RBT's promote an ethical atmosphere and make others aware of the PECC. RBTs ensure the ethical practice of behavior analysis. Specifically, they take the necessary actions to protect their clients if their clients are in harm's way, or they are aware of an ethical violation.

Public Statements (Code 8.0)

RBTs are truthful with respect to describing and presenting their work. They do not implement non-behavior analytic practices, and they do not promote non-behavior analytic services as being behavior analytic. For example, say that while you were in college you learned how to hypnotize people. Because the practice of hypnotizing people is not behavior analytic, our role as an RBT would *not* allow you to engage in such practices. In addition, RBTs only use trademarked or copyright material with permission and ensure appropriate credit to authors. If you are giving a presentation or training and utilizing material from another person's training, you must reference the original author. Regarding statements to and by others, RBTs promote positive statements regarding behavior analysis and include full disclosure (e.g., if you are being paid to make a statement you must disclose that you are being paid). More importantly, behavior analysts do NOT solicit or use testimonials of current clients or engage in uninvited in-person solicitation of business.

Behavior Analysis and Research (Code 9.0)

RBTs only engage in research that is consistent with laws and regulations. Moreover, RBTs do not falsify documentation, data, or report untruthful results or implications of research (omitting information constitutes untruthful reporting).

Behavior Analysts' Ethical Responsibility to the BACB (Code 10.0)

RBTs are truthful and honest in all documentation and applications submitted to the BACB. Thus, if inaccurate information has been submitted they immediately correct it. Moreover, RBTs must conform to all deadlines and do not infringe on the BACB's intellectual property (interventions and ideas created by the BCBA). RBTs adhere to all rules and regulations set out by the BACB, comply with supervision and coursework standards, are familiar with the PECC, and discourage misrepresentation by non-certified individuals. Specifically, you may not present yourself as a RBT or any kind of behavior analyst until you have the required course/content hours, pass the exam, and the competency assessment.

SUMMARY AND CONCLUSIONS

Basic professional codes ensure that professional and ethical guidelines are in place. This helps to ensure that the practice of a profession is in line with the best interests of clients. ABA accepts and includes such professional and ethical guidelines. Professional and ethical conduct is as important in practicing behavior analysis as understanding the concepts, procedures, and principles of behavior analysis. It is unrealistic to think you will never be in a position where you have to choose how to act one way or another. A big part of behaving ethically is not only knowing the code of ethics, but making sure you have the support and resources to behave ethically. *It is each RBT's responsibility to ensure they know the PECC and practice within the guidelines.*

EXERCISES

After you have completed the exercises below, you will want feedback. Your instructor has access (or can obtain access from the publisher) to sample answers for each of the following exercises:

For the following scenarios indicate which code is being violated, why, and what you could do differently.

1. Your supervisor develops a unique intervention that has not been empirically validated in the literature. Then, she tells you to implement it to decrease your client's problem behavior. Because it is your supervisor who asks you to implement it, you do.

2. You are working in a school and the teacher wants you to remove the client from the classroom, but it is not the procedure to implement according to the IEP and Behavior Support Plan. Because you want to maintain a friendly environment with the teacher, you take your client out of the classroom, which is in direct opposition to the intervention described in the plan, even though you know it is not in the best interest of the student you work with.

3. Because you work at multiple houses, you keep your clients' data on the front seat of your car.

4. It is your twenty-first birthday and you are very excited. You tell the mom of your client and at the end of the session she gives you $20 to buy yourself a drink later that evening.

5. Your friend is a marriage and family therapist and "taught" you how to implement a discounting procedure. You bring up the procedure up with the mom and say you want to implement it with her child during the behavior analysis sessions.

6. You have been working on a case for a while and really want to show improvement, but the client is just not improving. But you figure, "what the heck. If I just change the data a little, it will look like the client is improving and everyone will be happy." Thus, there really is no harm in changing the level of behavior just a little.

ACTIVITIES

1. Again, review the PECC on-line, and from each of the 10 sections state what you believe is the most important point or activity that it stipulates. Compare this to what another comes up with and come to a consensus.

Chapter 3

Introduction to Behavior Analysis Principles and Terms

GOALS

1. Define the terms behavior and analysis.
2. Where did principles of behavior analysis come from?
3. How is ABA related to principles of behavior analysis?
4. Describe what is meant by the A-B-Cs of behavior.
5. Describe what the difference is between positive and negative reinforcement.
6. Describe what is similar between positive and negative reinforcement.
7. Describe what the difference is between negative reinforcement and positive punishment.
8. Define extinction.
9. Describe what happens to the reinforcer during extinction.

10. Describe the difference between MOs and S^Ds.
11. Define prompts and stimulus control.
12. Provide the rational for including prompts to get someone to engage in behavior.
13. Complete this chapter's exercises/activities, or those assigned by your instructor.

*****

In Chapter 1 we described ABA as an area of behavior analysis and what it entails. Moreover, we discussed the concept that ABA is conceptually systematic, which means it utilizes procedures based upon the principles of behavior analysis. Being that what you will be doing is based upon these principles, it would be misguided to present only the procedures without giving you the foundation upon which those procedures are based. Although understanding these principles may not affect how well you implement the strategies in practice, you may understand the importance of implementing procedures with fidelity once you have some understanding of the principles behind them. The purpose of this chapter is to provide you with a basic understanding of the principles of behavior analysis. Because, the field of ABA utilizes very specific terms, and a brief review of the BACB's RBT task list can be somewhat overwhelming if you have never been acquainted with the behavior analysis vernacular, we feel it is important to break down the terms you will come across in your practicing ABA as well. On a cautionary note, this chapter is not intended to give you the conceptual expertise of a behavior analyst—it is meant as an introduction to avoid becoming lost when reading articles or chapters, going to conferences, or talking to behavior analysts.

To give a definition of behavior analysis, we put both of the words "behavior" and "analysis" into Wikipedia. In a nutshell, this is what came up:

> *Behavior* is the response of an organism to stimuli (anything that you can observe something doing or saying). *Analysis* is when you break down a complex topic into smaller parts to understand it.

So, behavior analysis is basically the process of understanding the principles of learning and behavior utilizing a scientific method. These principles of learning have been established from many years of scientific investigation in the area of the experimental analysis of behavior. In fact, there is a substantial body of research literature on how behavior is learned and changes over time. This body of literature is where we find basic principles of behavior analysis. The procedures we employ in ABA as an RBT, BCaBA or as a BCBA are based upon these behavioral principles that are known as evidence-based practices.

Basic Principles and Terms

In behavior analysis we study the **three-term contingency,** otherwise know as the A-B-C, where A is the antecedent (what happens right before the behavior and may have evoked or abated it), B is the behavior, and C is the consequence (what happens right after the behavior may increase or decrease the likelihood that the behavior will happen again). We try to determine how the A and the C affect the B. The ways in which the As and Cs affect the B are know as the *principles of behavior*. Typically, when presented with a choice of starting with the A or C in a sequence, we tend to start with the As. However, when explaining the principles of behavior in behavior analysis, the C is a great place to start.

Reinforcement

With respect to the Cs (or consequences) in behavior analysis, there are five principles that we want to go over. First, we will go over the principles of positive and negative reinforcement. The thing to remember here is that the words "positive" and "negative" only means whether something was added (positive) or removed (negative) following the behavior. Reinforcement has occurred if one of the following consequences leads to an increase in the behavior: something that is added due to the occurrence of a behavior or something is removed following a behavior. Think of math, where the "+" sign doesn't mean good, nor does the "−" sign mean bad. In behavior analysis, the positive and negative do not mean good or bad. They mean added or subtracted. Thus, *when something is added contingent on behavior and results in an increase in that behavior*, the principle underlying the procedure is **positive reinforcement**. Likewise, *when something is removed contingent on behavior and results in an increase in that behavior, the principle underlying the procedure* is **negative reinforcement**. Notice two things in the statements above: contingent on behavior and increases in behavior. Contingent on behavior means the contingency is related to the behavior, or its occurrence immediately precedes or follows the behavior. In this case, the contingency is the consequential delivery or removal of a stimulus when the behavior occurs. In both cases of reinforcement, the behavior increases, and the contingency is whether something was added or subtracted. Thus, we do not add or subtract the behavior itself. Regardless if a consequence is added or removed, the behavior always increases when reinforcement is used. Let's look at some examples: First, let's assume that the behavior increases after reinforcement is delivered.

A	B	C	+/– Reinforcement
Mom is holding a cookie.	Child says "Cookie."	Mom gives the child the cookie.	+ Reinforcement for saying cookie, cookie is delivered.
Michele nags at her partner to take the trash out.	Her partner takes the trash out.	Michele stops nagging.	– Reinforcement for taking out the trash (nagging is removed).
Dad puts child to bed.	Child starts crying and saying she had a bad dream.	Dad comes in and snuggles with her until she falls asleep.	+ Refinforcement for saying she had a bad dream and crying, she got got snuggles.
Teacher tells everyone to be quiet while taking their tests.	Johnny starts making siren sounds.	The whole class starts laughing and giving Johnny attention.	+ Reinforcement for making siren sounds (even seemingly unfavorable attention can be reinforcing) he got attention.

Table continued on next page

A	B	C	+/– **Reinforcement**
Hillary asks her son to clean up his room.	AJ starts holding his tummy and complaining of a tummy ache.	Hillary tells her son that he can clean his room later when he feels better.	– Reinforcement for saying his tummy hurts, he got out of cleaning the room or the demand to clean the room was removed.

Punishment

The next two principles are very similar to positive and negative reinforcement, but they result in a decrease in behavior. They are called positive and negative punishment (unlike how we think of the word punishment in everyday use, here it simply means the behavior decreases as a result of the consequence). *Remember, the positive and negative just tell us if something is added or removed, and not if something is good or bad.* Thus, in **positive punishment**, *an aversive (undesired) stimulus is added following the behavior, which reduces the likelihood of that behavior occurring in the future.* In **negative punishment**, *a reinforcing (or desired) stimulus is removed contingent on behavior, which results in a decrease in the future probability of that behavior.* Note that word "contingent" again, and in both cases behavior is reduced. *Therefore, the word "punishment" in behavior analysis means, when a behavior progressively decreases due to something systematically being added or taken away following the behavior's occurrence*, not that you are getting retribution for the misappropriate behavior. Let's look at some examples of both positive and negative punishment: Let's assume in the examples on the next page that the given behavior will decrease in the future.

A	B	C	+/– Reinforcement
Paul is mad at his mom.	He hits and kicks his mother.	His Mom tells him he cannot watch TV for the rest of the night.	– Punishment for hitting and kicking, the TV was removed.
The speed limit sign read 35 miles per hour.	Marty is driving 65 miles per hour.	The cop pulls Marty over and gives him a $200 ticket.	– Punishment (this was tricky because he got a ticket, but getting the ticket cost him money).
April is wearing a device that delivers a small shock when she hits her head	April hits her head with her fist.	The device delivers a shock.	+ Punishment for hitting her head, the shock is delivered
Jamie is chewing gum.	Jamie puts her chewed gum under the desk at school.	The teacher makes her clean all of the desks in the school.	+ Punishment for placing gum under desk, cleaning is added

Here are two charts to help you with the similarities and differences between positive reinforcement, negative reinforcement, positive punishment, and negative punishment. Use whichever one works best for you.

	Behavior Increases	*Behavior Decreases*
Stimulus Added	**Positive Reinforcement**	**Positive Punishment**
Stimulus Removed	**Negative Reinforcement**	**Negative Punishment**

Positive Punishment	**Negative Punishment**	**Positive Reinforcement**	**Negative Reinforcement**
Consequence Added	*Consequence Subtracted*	*Consequencee Added*	*Consequence Subtracted*
Behavior decreases	Behavior decreases	Behavior increases or maintains	Behavior increases or maintains

Note that the only difference between punishment and reinforcement is the effect the consequence has on the likelihood the behavior will happen again in the future. For one child, the consequence might be being yelled at. If the behavior decreases, the yelling was punishing. If the behavior increases, the yelling was reinforcing (probably due to the attention it provided). ALWAYS look at the effect the consequence (or the reaction) has on the behavior before calling it reinforcement or punishment.

Extinction

The next *C* we are going to discuss is a principle called *extinction*, which leads to a decrease or elimination of the behavior when applied. Now, the thing with extinction is that reinforcement has to be occurring before extinction can be implemented. The definition of **extinction** *is the discontinuation of reinforcement (positive or negative), which is contingent on a behavior that leads to a decrease in that behavior*. Simply speaking, extinction occurs when you have a behavior that is being reinforced via positive or negative reinforcement, and you stop delivering the reinforcer. You either don't deliver the positive reinforcer, or you don't remove the aversive event. By doing this you eliminate the reinforcing contingency, which leads to a decrease in behavior. Let's look at the examples above of positive and negative reinforcement and how you would implement extinction.

A	B	C	+/– Reinforcement	Extinction
Mom is holding a cookie.	Child says "Cookie."	Mom gives the child the cookie.	+ Reinforcement	Mom does not give cookie when child says "Cookie."
Michele nags at her partner to take the trash out.	Her partner takes the trash out.	Michele stopped nagging.	– Reinforcement	Michele keeps nagging.

Table continued on next page

A	B	C	+/– **Reinforcement**	Extinction
Dad puts child to bed.	Child starts crying and saying she had a bad dream.	Dad comes in and snuggles with her until she falls asleep.	+ Reinforcement	Dad doesn't say anything and puts the child back to bed.
Teacher tells everyone to be quiet while taking their tests	Johnny starts making siren sounds	The whole class starts laughing and giving Johnny atten-ion	+ Reinforcement	Class no longer laughs or gives Johnny attention.
Hillary asks her son to clean up his room.	AJ starts holding his tummy and comlaining of a tummy ache.	Hillary tells her son that he can clean his room later when he feels better.	– Reinforcement	Hillary makes her son clean the room.

One thing that is important to note is defining these principles and terms is by no means a complete conceptual explanation. However, we feel that by introducing these key principles and terms, you will know their meanings when someone talks about reinforcement, punishment, and extinction that is based upon how the *B* changes given the *C*.

Stimulus Control and Motivational Operations

There are two key areas of the *A*s we would like to cover: discriminative stimuli and motivating operations (MOs). Basically, **discriminative stimuli** (S^Ds) are *antecedents that affect behavior* by signaling what will happen following a behavior (the *A* that signals the expectation of a certain *C*). **Motivating operations** affect the potency (how rewarding or aversive something is) of the contingencies (consequences and antecedents related to the behavior's occurrence). Let's tackle the discriminative stimuli first. The first thing to understand is that *when an antecedent stimulus gains control or influence over behavior, we call this* **stimulus control.** Stimulus control can develop naturally or be programmed by a behavior analyst. The "control" it exerts can be to signal that reinforcement will be delivered contingent on behavior, extinction (the cessation of reinforcement) will occur, or punishment will occur contingent on behavior. This control is learned by consistently experiencing the same consequences for each behavior evoked by a certain S^D. For example, every day a teacher denies the students access to lunch (the reinforcer, or *C*) until their work area is clear (*B*). Thus, the lunch bell (the S^D or *A*) signals the opportunity for reinforcement, so the students clean their desks to earn their learned reward. Moreover, how well these antecedent stimuli control behavior is on a continuum from tight stimulus control (*stimulus discrimination*) or loose stimulus control (*stimulus generalization*). One is not necessarily better than the other, and its success depends on the outcome you desire. For example, if you only want a child to call her mother "mommy," you will need tight stimulus control. However, if you want the same child to greet others with a smile and "hello," you will need loose stimulus control. Specific procedures for developing or extinguishing stimulus control will be presented throughout this book when we talk about increasing and decreasing behavior. For the time being, you should know that antecedent stimuli are able to control behavior by signaling what consequence will follow behavior.

The other *A* we would like to talk about is the MO (a.k.a., establishing operations). Basically, the **MO** affects behavior by altering the potency (or reinforcing value) of the consequence and antecedent and either establishing or abolishing their effects. Generally speaking, reinforcement is about states of **deprivation** or **satiation**. Specifically, *if I am deprived of a reinforcer, it makes the reinforcer more potent. However, if I am satiated on the reinforcer, then it makes the reinforcer less potent. Thus, I am more inclined to engage in the behavior when the reinforcer is more potent than when it is less potent.* Likewise, MOs affect the potency of punishment as well. For example, if my environment is aversive, it actually abolishes the potency of punishment. However, if my environment is enjoyable, it establishes the potency of punishment. Let's look at the similarities and differences before we move on.

	S^Ds	MOs
Similar	Antecedent Stimulus	Antecedent Stimulus
Different	Controls behavior by signalling consequence	Controls behavior by altering potency of consequence and antecedent.
*S^Ds = discriminative stimuli, MOs = motivating operations		

Prompts

There is a third *A* that is needed sometimes to get an individual to engage in the behavior. They are called prompts. Sometimes, we will have to temporarily introduce and subsequently fade out prompts. **Prompts** are not the MO, nor are they the preferred or the natural S^D. *When using prompts, you are substituting an effective but inappropriate S^D for an ineffective but appropriate S^D.* In fact, our end goal is to produce the behavior without providing prompts. However, sometimes in the beginning of programs we need prompts to ensure we get the behavior we want to reinforce. There are different kinds of prompts we can use, including: adding reminders, examples, instructions, imitative prompts, rules, and even physical guidance. The important thing to remember is that you do not want them entering into the contingency permanently or the occurrence of the behavior to be dependent on prompts. When presented with "the problem" (the natural S^D), you want your client to solve it without it being requested, shown, or instructed how to do it. There will be more on the different types of prompts and how to use them later.

Additional Terms and Acronyms

As you read through the above text, you might have felt the need for a dictionary for words such as cessation, evoke, potency, and many more. It is not our intent to use difficult language and in most places we have avoided such language when describing principles and procedures. However, sometimes words really make a difference and we think it is best to learn the correct words associated with different principles from the start than trying to relearn later on. With that said, we know firsthand that learning about ABA is like learning a new language. So, before we get started on that journey, we thought it might be a good idea to go over some behavior analysis terminology and commonly used acronyms. Most of the following terms will be introduced more thoroughly in subsequent chapters.

S^{r+}: Positive Reinforcement—Delivery of a stimulus (reinforcing or desired) contingent on behavior that increases the occurrence of that behavior.

S^{r-}: Negative Reinforcement—Removal of a stimulus (aversive or undesired) contingent on behavior that increases the occurrence of that behavior.

Pun+: Positive Punishment—Delivery of a stimulus (aversive or undesired) contingent on behavior that decreases the occurrence of that behavior.

Pun–: Negative Punishment—Removal of a stimulus (reinforcing or desired) contingent on behavior that decreases the occurrence of that behavior.

EXT: Extinction—Discontinuation of reinforcement contingent on a behavior that reduces that behavior.

S^{Dr}: Discriminative Stimulus for Reinforcement—A stimulus that signals if the client responds with a specific behavior, reinforcement will occur.

S^{Δ}: Discriminative Stimulus for Extinction—A stimulus that signals if the client responds with a specific behavior, reinforcement will not occur.

S^{Dp}: Discriminative Stimulus for Punishment—A stimulus that signals if the client responds with a specific behavior, punishment will occur.

MO: Motivating Operation—An antecedent stimulus that alters the potency of the consequence and the immediate antecedent.

FR: Fixed Ratio Schedule of Reinforcement—A schedule in which a reinforcer is delivered based upon the number of responses, and the number does not vary.

VR: Variable Ratio Schedule of Reinforcement—A schedule in which a reinforcer is delivered based upon the number of responses, and the number varies from reinforcer to reinforcer.

FI: Fixed Interval Schedule of Reinforcement—A schedule in which a reinforcer is delivered based upon the first response after a given time period, and the time period remains the same.

VI: Variable Interval Schedule of Reinforcement—A schedule in which a reinforcer is delivered based upon the first response after a given time period, and the time period varies from one reinforcer to another.

FT: Fixed Time Schedule—A schedule where a consequence is delivered after a certain amount of time noncontingent of behavior (meaning based upon time, not whether or not a behavior occurred).

VT: Variable Time Schedule—A schedule where a consequence is delivered after a varied amount of time noncontingent of behavior. The time varies from consequence to consequence.

BACB: Behavior Analysis Certification Board—The board that oversees the certification of behavior analyst.

BCBA: Board Certified Behavior Analyst—A person who is certified through the BACB who has a master's degree, completed the required course work and supervision, and has passed the certification exam.

BCaBA: Board Certified Assistant Behavior Analyst—A person who is certified through the BACB who has a bachelor's degree, completed the required course work and supervision, and has passed the certification exam.

RBT: Registered Behavior Technician—A person who is certified through the BACB who has a high school diploma, completed the required course work and supervision, and has passed the registration exam.

BL: Baseline—Level of behavioral performance before manipulation of environmental stimuli (antecedents or consequences). Behavior as it typically occurs prior to the intervention or treatment.

TX: Treatment—Level of behavioral performance while manipulations of environmental stimuli are occurring.

A: Antecedent Stimulus—the stimulus that occurs prior to the behavior, including S^Ds and MOs.

B: Behavior—Actions, including saying and doing.

C: Consequence—the contingency that occurs after the behavior.

TB: Target Behavior—the behavior of interest, or the behavior to be changed.

DRO: Differential Reinforcement of Other Behavior—delivery of a reinforcer contingent on the absence of the TB.

DRA: Differential Reinforcement of Alternative Behavior—delivery of a reinforcer contingent on an alternative behavior

Data—The results of measuring the TB.

Social Reinforcer—A reinforcer that is either delivered or removed by another person.

Automatic Reinforcer—A reinforcer that is inherent in the response itself.

SUMMARY AND CONCLUSIONS

Given that all behavior analytic procedures are based upon the principles of behavior analysis, this chapter introduced a number of basic principles, such as: positive and negative reinforcement; positive and negative punishment; extinction; and the difference between MOs and discriminative stimuli. Moreover, a number of specific acronyms and definitions of terms were presented to help familiarize you with the terminology used within behavior analysis. How to use these principles to change behavior will be further discussed throughout the book when we cover specific interventions for understanding behavior, increasing and teaching adaptive behavior, and for decreasing problem behavior.

EXERCISES

After you have completed the matching below, you will want feedback. Your instructor has access (or can obtain access from the publisher) to sample answers for each of the following exercises:

Match:

Motivating Operation	A. Removal of a stimulus contingent on behavior that decreases the occurrence of that behavior.
FR	B. The behavior of interest.
Consequence	C. Discontinuation of reinforcement contingent on a behavior that reduces that behavior.
Automatic Reinforcer	D. Baseline
A	E. The contingency that occurs after the behavior.
S^{DP}	F. A stimulus that signals if organism responds punishment will occur.
Negative Punishment	G. An antecedent stimulus that alters the potency of the consequence and antecedent.
Extinction	H. A reinforcer that is inherent in the response itself.
BL	I. Antecedent Stimulus
TP	J. Fixed Ratio Schedule of Reinforcement.

ACTIVITY

1. Pair up with another person who is preparing to become an RBT (or even an BCaBA or BCBA) and observe others in their natural environments. Identify what behavior procedures are being used in the natural environment (including positive and negative reinforcement, positive and negative punishment, extinction, discriminative stimuli, and motivational operations) and compare notes. Discuss your results with one another. If you unable to agree, confer with a BCBA. Or, if you do not have access to another who is preparing to become an RBT,

> or who knows ABA, do the observation in your own living or work setting.
>
> 2. Make flashcards of all the terms and definitions in this chapter and keep going through them until you can get them all correct within one minute.

Chapter 4

Measuring Behavior

GOALS

1. Describe what it means to provide an operational definition of a behavior.
2. Discuss why it is important to operationalize a behavior.
3. Give an operational definition for (a) tantrums, (b) incorrect responses, and (c) disruption.
4. Define and illustrate permanent product recording.
5. Define and illustrate the following observational procedures: (a) frequency or event recording, (b) duration recording, and (c) latency recording.
6. Behaviors must meet certain conditions before one can use event, duration or latency to measure them. Discuss what those conditions are.

7. List, define, and illustrate the three interval measurement systems.
8. Complete this chapter's exercises/activities, or those assigned by your instructor.

*****

As an RBT, one of the biggest parts of your job will be to measure behavior. In this chapter, we will walk you through how to select behavior to measure and develop operational definitions. We will provide an overview of basic measurement systems and how to select the best one for specific target behaviors. Also, we will discuss what reliability is, how to conduct and report on interobserver agreement, and how to ensure objective and reliable measurement throughout your sessions.

Selecting and Operationally Defining Behavior for Change

Given that ABA focuses on producing predictable and replicable improvements in socially significant behavior that result in long-lasting change, picking the *right* behavior to target for measurement and change is extremely important. It is best to get it right the first time rather than to embark on a behavior change program and a month later realize you picked the wrong behavior. There are a number of things to take into account when selecting behavior for change: a) Whose behavior is being targeted and why? b) What is the likelihood of the behavior producing natural reinforcement? c) Is there access to important environments? d) Is the behavior a prerequisite to other behavior? e) Is the targeted behavior age appropriate? f) Will it produce direct benefits (short- and long-term reinforcers, and minimize short- and long-term punishers) for the client and others? After selecting the behavior for change, you must operationally define the behavior. Defining a behavior operationally ensures that everyone is targeting and measuring the same behavior and prevents any feelings or assumptions the observer may have about the client from influencing the data.

Developing an operational definition of the target behavior will contain a number of criteria. For example, it must be: a) clear and unambiguous; b) objective (i.e., observable characteristics void of inferential terms, based upon inferences of mental capacity); and c) complete (i.e., includes what actions do and don't count as occurrences of the target behavior). Let's look at some examples and practice developing operational definitions. Remember these definitions must be clear, objective, and complete. After you read the example, ask yourself the following questions: a) Could you act out the behavior as defined? b) Is it clear, and do you know what the definition means? c) Is it objective (meaning, is it observable) and not based upon mental states (e.g., being mad, frustrated, etc.)? d) Is it complete, and does it include what will count and not count? Ask yourself the same questions once you define the target behaviors (can you act it out, and is it clear, objective, and complete?).

TABLE 4.1 Operational Definitions

Target Behavior	Operational Definition
Aggression	Any instance of Jack hitting, kicking, or pushing others
Self-injurious Behavior	Any instance of Terry bringing her hand to her head and making forceful contact. Gently touching her face or head does not count.
Correct Responses	When given the S^D, Sarah engages in the defined behavior within 5 seconds without prompting.

Given that one of the main duties of an RBT is to measure behavior, you must ensure that you are working off an operational definition. This ensures that the behavior you are measuring is the behavior of interest. After the target behavior(s) have been selected and operationally defined, the next step is to select a measurement procedure.

SELECTING MEASUREMENT SYSTEMS

In behavior analysis, we put a lot of stock in the accurate measuring of the target behavior. Thus, measurement systems must include the following: record ongoing performance (not based on memory), be reliable (i.e., consistent and results are easily replicated no matter who is recording), be valid (i.e., accurate), be sensitive, incorporate dimensional (as opposed to binary measurement), and measure relevant aspects of the target behavior. There are a number of common measurement systems utilized in behavioral programs, including: outcome (product), frequency, duration, latency, and interval measures (e.g., whole-interval, partial-interval, and momentary time sampling). Each of these measurement systems is associated with benefits as well as limitations. Moreover, there are specific justifications for choosing one measurement system over another. Given that you may be required to record behavior using one of these common methods, let's look at how to utilize each of these recording methods.

Permanent Product Measurement

When using **outcome** (or **permanent product**) recording, you are measuring the result or how many times the individual engaged in the behavior. Permanent product recording is used to measure behavior that leaves behind physical proof of its occurrance, so you can record or justify the accuracy of your data later. For example, you might count the number of math problems completed on a test, puzzles completed, or marks on walls. In any event, you are recording the product or aftermath of the individual engaging in the behavior. Here is an example (see Figure 4.1) of using a frequency measure to record the number of math problems completed, and an example of where you would put a tally mark in the box corresponding to the number of math problems for each day of the week:

Figure 4.1

Day of the Week	Number of Math Problems Completed
Monday	IIIII
Tuesday	III
Wednesday	III
Thursday	IIIII
Friday	IIIIIII
TOTAL FOR WEEK:	23

Process Measurement—Frequency

Rather than recording the outcome, with frequency, duration, and latency measures, you are recording the process (or ongoing behavior). You may record the following when taking **frequency** data: the number of times someone does a particular behavior, the number of times they did a particular behavior during a specified period of time (i.e., rate), or the number of times they engaged in the behavior when given a certain number of opportunities (i.e., percentage opportunity). Frequency data should be considered when the time a behavior starts and ends is clear (e.g., discrete behaviors). The thing to remember is that you are interested in counting the number of times a behavior occurs. However, be aware that event or frequency recording can only be used if each instance the behavior is measured is roughly equivalent in durations. For example, let's take temper tantrums (yelling, throwing things, refusing to do as told, etc,). Your baseline might show 3 or 4 instances during a session. Once your intervention started, it reduced to one instance during the session. That may looks like an improvement, but not if that one instance lasted the entire session. That is why each occurrence must be roughly equivalent in duration to use this observational procedure. Here is an example of using a frequency measure (see Figure 4.2 on the next page) to record the number of aggressive behaviors using a pre-numbered data sheet. All you need to do is circle or strike out the number every time the person was aggressive.

A lot of times you just want to know how often a behavior happens, thus simple tallies on a paper or using clickers can really be convenient. For example, let's say I want to know how many times Johnny greets a customer before taking his order at the local burger shop. I could wear a finger clicker and push the button every time he greets a customer and a different clicker for every time he takes an order, then divide the number of greets by the number of orders to get the percentage of opportunity. I could also simply put a mark on a paper every time Maddy starts repeating the phrase "butter toast" to get a count of how many times she says it per day. Recording frequency is very convenient when you can tell when the behavior starts, when it stops, and when it lasts for about the same time every time it happens.

Figure 4.2

Day — Date	Aggression	Total per Day
Monday	1 2 3 4 5 6 7 8 9 10 11 12 13 14 15 16 17 18 19 20	
Tuesday	1 2 3 4 5 6 7 8 9 10 11 12 13 14 15 16 17 18 19 20	
Wednesday	1 2 3 4 5 6 7 8 9 10 11 12 13 14 15 16 17 18 19 20	
Thursday	1 2 3 4 5 6 7 8 9 10 11 12 13 14 15 16 17 18 19 20	
Friday	1 2 3 4 5 6 7 8 9 10 11 12 13 14 15 16 17 18 19 20	
Saturday	1 2 3 4 5 6 7 8 9 10 11 12 13 14 15 16 17 18 19 20	
Sunday	1 2 3 4 5 6 7 8 9 10 11 12 13 14 15 16 17 18 19 20	
TOTAL		M=

Process Measurement—Duration

When using **duration**, you are measuring the amount of time that passes from the onset of the behavior until the offset of the behavior. In other words, you are measuring how long the behavior lasts. Here is an example of duration recording of tantrums (See Figure 4.3):

Some likely situations where you might want to record duration are: the amount of time it takes someone to finish a meal or complete their homework; how long someone works out; or how long someone

Figure 4.3

Date of Tantrum	Start Time	End Time	Total Duration
11/3/16	10;30 am	10:45 am	15 minutes
11/3/16	12:11 am	12:45 am	34 minutes
11/5/16	9:20 am	10:00 am	40 minutes
			M = 30 minutes

takes for a work break. In all of these examples, recording how long with a timer would work perfectly.

Process Measurement—Latency

Duration and latency are both interested in recording time, but latency is concerned with the amount of time from when antecedent stimulus (such as a request) is given to the onset of the response (see Figure 4.4). It should be obvious through event, duration, and latency measures that you can only use these measurement systems if you can tell when each instance of the behavior starts and stops.

Figure 4.4

Trial	S^D "let's work" presented at	Onset of Response	Total Duration
Trial 1	7:15 am	7:25 am	10 minutes
Trial 2	9:30 am	9:35 am	5 minutes
Trial 3	10:00 am	10:17 am	17 minutes
Trial 4	11:00 am	11:08	8 minutes
			M = 10 minutes

Recording how long it takes someone to respond, such as starting chores or homework, can be very important, especially if it is taking too long to happen. A lot of things in life require short reaction times, thus being able to measure how long it takes someone to react can be useful. As mentioned earlier, the behavior must be discrete: have clearly observable starting and ending points. This is not a concern with interval measurement, our next topic.

Interval Measurement

When using interval measurement procedures, you record whether behavior occurred or did not occur during a specified interval depending on the type of interval recording you are using. With *whole* interval recording, you record if the behavior occurred throughout the entire interval. This is used primarily for behaviors that you want to increase (e.g., sitting and attending). However, with *partial* interval recording, you record if the behavior occurred at any time within the interval. This is used primarily for behaviors that you want to decrease (e.g., hitting and self-injurious behaviors). With *momentary time sampling*, you record whether the behavior is occurring at the end of the interval. These methods do not require that the behavior being recorded be discrete. However, whole and partial interval recording do take considerable time, and should only be used if recommended or approved by your supervisor (BCBA or BCaBA). In other words, The BCBA or BCaBA on the case should select the specific measurement system, develop the system of how you will record behavior, and monitor your recording (e.g., train you on the recording method, conduct interobserver checks, etc.). Here is an example of interval recording, where in the data collector scored the interval as the behavior occurring, by placing a X in the interval, when the behavior occurred at the end of the interval (See Figure 4.5):

Figure 4.5

39/60 = % INTERVALS	0–10s	11–20s	21–30s	31–40s	41–50s	51–60s
	X		X		X	X
1+	X			X	X	X
2+	X	X	X	X		X
3+	X	X		X		X
4+	X		X		X	
5+		X	X	X	X	X
6+		X		X		
7+	X	X	X		X	X
8+	X		X	X	X	
9+		X		X		X

Implementing Measurement Systems

Measurement systems can be housed on smart phones, laptops, automated systems, or paper and pencil. The examples above represent using paper and pencil to record data about behavior. Whichever method you have chosen to collect data, it is important that the data collector is trained on the measurement system and that the RBT has collected data on the client for a sufficient time to avoid reactivity (i.e., adaptation period, or a client's reaction to the act of being observed rather than the intervention itself). Just as your own behavior might change if someone is watching you, so might the client's behavior as well. Thus, it is important to record data on the client until all reactivity has been eliminated and prior to taking baseline or assessment levels of performance.

SUMMARY AND CONCLUSIONS

Selecting behavior for change, defining it, and utilizing the appropriate measurement system is the crux of what we do in behavior analysis. We cannot tell what effect our intervention is having on a behavior without such assessment. Thus, the importance of these procedures cannot be glossed over. It is important to determine if the target behavior is operationally defined before starting to measure the behavior. Subsequently, it is important to understand how to record the behavior with the appropriate measurement system. It is important to understand the way in which you record a behavior using the different measurement systems of outcome, frequency, duration, latency, and interval recording, so you record both reliable and valid measures of the behavior (see Chapter 5 for how to assess for reliability and validity). In addition to being sufficiently trained on the implementation of the measurement system, it is important that the client adapts to having their behavior recorded.

EXERCISES

After you have completed the exercises below, you will want feedback. Your instructor has access (or can obtain access from the publisher) to sample answers for each of the following exercises:

1. What measurement system is used to measure behavior after the behavior has occurred?

2. Which process measurement system is utilized to measure the amount of time it takes before the behavior occurs after a specific stimulus?
3. Which observation method would you use for each of the following behaviors?
   a. tantrum (yelling, screaming, crying, hitting)
   b. doing homework
   c. fights
   d. assignments handed in to teacher
   e. giving compliments
   f. paying attention
   g. sucking on thumb (thumb touching mouth)
   h. number of sentences written
   i. a baby crying

ACTIVITIES

1. Observe your own behavior that is sort of a habit (like biting your nails, saying "you know," etc.), operationally define the behavior, select a measurement system and justify its use, develop the measurement system, and record its occurrence.

2. Go to a local coffee shop or bar and pick someone who keeps doing the same behavior over and over. For example, someone checking their phone or eating nuts out of a bowl. Select a measurement system and measure the behavior for 10 minutes. What did you learn from this experience?

Chapter 5

Reporting Behavioral Data

GOALS

1. Define reliable and valid measures of behavior.
2. Describe how validity is assessed in behavior analysis. Describe the difference between validity and reliability.
3. Express the formulas used to calculate reliability using Total Agreement, Interval Agreement, and Occurrence/Nonoccurrence Agreement.
4. Discuss some threats to reliability and how to correct them.
5. Describe under what circumstances you would use a line vs. a bar vs. a standard celeration chart (SCC) graph.
6. Make and plot a line graph and a bar graph.
7. Complete this chapter's exercises/activities, or those assigned by your instructor.

*****

As you know from the previous chapter, measurement of behaviors is extremely important in behavior change programs. In ABA, *we deter-*

mine if we are effective or not by analyzing data. To emphasize the importance of this point, a court decision regarding the use of timeout for a student stated that not only must a baseline (i.e., repeated measure of the behavior before intervention) be collected before using timeout, but the frequency of the problem behavior had to show a decrease after intervention. Thus, because the teachers did not have data to demonstrate the effectiveness of timeout, it was deemed not to be an appropriate intervention for the student and was not defensable. The judge's stipulation follows good ABA practice. However, before we analyze the data to make treatment decisions, we must make sure the data are both reliable and valid. **Reliable** means the data are consistent (meaning each recorder is recording the same behavior the same way) and repeatable, while **valid** means the data are accurate and represent the behavior we are measuring (e.g., using ounces to measure weight vs. inches). Both are important in behavior analysis, but we generally make a determination of validity by way of reliability. If the measurement is reliable, we assume it is valid. However, we must point out the problem with this assumption, even though it is the assumption we work off of. For example, you put a ruler in a pot of boiling water. If you ask two observers to measure the temperature, they will likely produce repeatable measures. However, measuring inches of water does not equal temperature. Similarly, you set up a goal to increase your client's paying attention by reliably measuring eye contact. Is eye contact a valid measure of paying attention? NO! It's only part of paying attention. Paying attention could also include answering questions, asking questions, nodding head, etc. So, just because you have reliability, does not guarantee that you also have validity. However, you cannot have validity without reliability. For example, when you get on a scale to measure your weight and one time it reports you weigh 130 pounds, and later in the day it reports you weigh 180, you cannot conclude that it is measuring your weight accurately. Because the data were not reliable and showed inconsistency in its weight measurements, it cannot be considered a valid or an accurate measurement of your weight. Always make sure that you have reliability and are measuring what you report you are measuring. In summary then, when we talk about reliability we are usually talking about two independent observers recording the same degree of occurrence of the behavior. Our measures are valid if they are reliable and are measuring what we claim to measure.

ASSESSING FOR RELIABILITY AND VALIDITY

You may be wondering how we know if a measure is repeatable and consistent. We assess reliability in behavior analysis by recording, calculating, and reporting ***interobserver agreement* (IOA)**. IOA is the measure of how well two observers agree when measuring behavior by comparing how well the results of both observers match when recording the same behavior at the same time. Let's start with the recording part. When recording IOA you will have two observers collecting data using the developed measurement system during the same observation period. The important thing is to remember that the observers cannot confer with each other while recording data. They must record behavior independently. Thus, observer one cannot ask observer two, "Did you see that?" or, "Did you score that as the behavior?" You can ask such questions after data collection has been completed and the reliability calculated. Such discussions are encouraged in that they help improve IOA. In fact, it is a good routine to have a conversation before the observation to ensure that you and the other observer are using the same behavioral definition. Then if IOA is weak, it might be beneficial to have an extended conversation to clarify what behaviors fall under the exact operational definition of the target behavior being measured. Then, the behavior analyst can change the definition to avoid future confusion.

The recommendation for the amount of IOA you should get is 33% of all observation sessions. Thus, if you are recording behavior on Monday, Wednesday, and Friday, you must have a second observer record data at the same time at least one of those days. Some agencies might say, "we cannot record IOA for 33% of the sessions, because it is too costly." However, we would like to point out that we assume validity based upon reliability. Thus, if we are not recording adequate amounts of reliability, how can we assume that our measures are valid? There are ways to get around having to schedule two observers at the same time. One way is to video record the session and have a second observer record data off the video recording. Another way is to live stream the session, so the second observer can record data as the session is occurring. Either way, we cannot stress how important it is to ensure that IOA is being recorded, and that decisions about behavioral programming are made from reliable measures.

The next step to ensure we are making decisions with reliable and valid information is to assess the extent the two independent observers are using the same measuring tool, observing the same instance of behavior, and agreeing with each other's data. There are a couple of common methods for calculating IOA, and the specific method utilized is dependent on the measurement system being utilized. The most common methods are total, interval, and *occurrence/nonoccurrence* agreement.

Total agreement is expressed as the percentage of agreement between the total amounts of behavior recorded by two independent observers. Find the percentage of agreement by utilizing the formula: *smaller/larger X 100*. The higher the percent determined by this calculation, the greater the likelihood that the data are valid and reliable. This type of agreement is used to calculate IOA for frequency, rate, duration, latency, and IRT measures (described in Chapter 4). For example, observer 1 recorded that the behavior occurred 10 times during the observation period, and the second observer recorded behavior as occurring 15 times. You would calculate IOA by dividing 10 by 15 and multiplying the sum by 100 (IOA = 66.7%) *Before moving on to other calculations, it is important to note that 66.7% IOA is weak; more about this in a minute.* What about a duration example? What would you do if observer 1 said the behavior lasted for 24 minutes, and observer 2 said the behavior lasted for 20 minutes? How would you calculate IOA?[1]

Interval agreement is expressed as the percentage of agreement between the intervals, in which two independent observers agree that behavior did or did not occur. Find the percent of agreement by utilizing the formula: *number of agreed upon intervals/number of agreed and disagreed upon intervals X 100*. Interval agreement is unique, because it does not represent the exact frequency of the behavior. This type of agreement is used to calculate IOA for whole-interval, partial-interval, and momentary time sampling measures. Let's look at the example on the next page.

---

[1] 20/24 = 0.833 X 100 = 83.3% IOA

Figure 5.1

	0–10s	11–20s	21–30s	31–40s	41–50s	51–60s
1+	X		X		X	X
2+	X	X		X	X	X
3+	X		X		X	
4+	X	X	X	X	X	X
5+		X	X	X	X	X
6+		X		X		
7+	X	X	X		X	X
8+	X		X	X	X	
9+		X	X	X		X

	0–10s	11–20s	21–30s	31–40s	41–50s	51–60s
1+	X		X	X		X
2+	X		X	X	X	X
3+	X	X		X	X	
4+	X	X	X		X	X
5+		X	X	X	X	X
6+		X	X		X	
7+	X		X	X	X	X
8+	X		X		X	
9+		X	X			X

In this example, the highlighted boxes indicate the intervals in which the two observers agreed. There are 51 highlighted intervals, and the total number of intervals is 60. Thus, to calculate interval agreement you would take the 51 intervals, divide it by 60 intervals, and multiple by 100 (IOA = 85% of the intervals). FYI: *In this example, the IOA is sufficient. Let's look at another example.* If observer 1 and observer 2 agreed that Mark was on-task for 15 intervals and off-task for 10 intervals out of a total of 30 intervals, how would you calculate IOA?[2] If you have either high rates or really low rates of behavior when calculating reliability, you will only use unscored intervals (for high rates behavior) and scored intervals (for low rate behavior) in an effort to be more stringent with your analyses of reliability.

Occurrence/nonoccurrence agreement is expressed as the amount that two observers agreed that behavior did or didn't occur. This amount is calculated by utilizing the formula: agreements/disagreements + agreements X 100. If you are measuring whether or not a behavior occurred or didn't occur, then this method is how you would calculate IOA. It differs from a total agreement in that an occurrence/nonoccurrence agreement can only measure events and evaluates the agreement of the behavior's absents, while a total agreement can measure time and occurrences without examining the absents of behavior. For example, you would use this type of agreement when measuring whether or not Hillary took her medicine every day for a week. Observer 1 (Hillary's mom) said she took it Monday, Tuesday, Thursday, Saturday, and Sunday, and observer 2 (Hillary's dad) said she took it Monday, Tuesday, Thursday, and Sunday. They agreed on the occurrence of the behavior Monday, Tuesday, Thursday and Sunday and agreed on the nonoccurrence on Wednesday and Friday. Thus, you would calculate IOA by taking occurrence + non-occurrence agreement (6), dividing it by the agreements + disagreement (7), and multiplying by 100 = 85.7%. *FYI: 85.7% is adequate IOA.*

After you record and analyze IOA, how do you report it? IOA is always expressed as the percentage of agreement. When reporting the actual IOA, you also report the percentage of IOA recorded during the span of that observation period. For example, I am reporting IOA for

---

[2] 25 agreed upon intervals/30 = 0.833 X 100 = 83.3%.

the month of May (e.g. the observation period). If I recorded IOA on 10 out of 20 days, I would state in the report that IOA was recorded for 50% of the sessions. Rather than reporting each individual IOA score, I would report the mean from all of the sessions in which I took IOA. Looking at the example above, let's say that for the 10 sessions IOA was recorded the scores were 95%, 99%, 100%, 85%, 90%, 98% 90% 95%, 97% and 100%. I would report that IOA was recorded for 50% of the sessions and that the mean IOA was 94.9% (sum of scores divided by the number of scores = mean of scores). It also is helpful to report the range (e.g., 85% to 100%) in addition to the mean of the scores to let others know how your data varied. You may be thinking, "What is an acceptable mean of IOA?" Most would agree the higher the better. Generally, as long as the mean is above 85% there is no need to worry. However, if IOA drops lower than 85%, there is likely a problem that needs to be addressed. Some threats to reliability are problems with the measurement system (e.g., too complex or behavior not clearly operationalized), inadequate observer training, and unintended influences such as observer expectations. If IOA falls below 85%, the BCBA or BCaBA supervising the case must get to the bottom of the problem. They can fix it by either making the measurement system less complex, re-training the observers, or discussing how one's expectations can affect observation (include how dangerous that can be in a behavioral program).

Graphing Behavioral Data

Besides reporting IOA, the actual target behavior needs to be recorded as well. In the last chapter, we briefly described how you would report the data based upon the measurement system selected. Besides reporting the summary of the data in numerical format, behavior analysis relies on visual inspection of graphs to determine effects. Thus, you must take the data you recorded, and graph it so that a BCBA or BCaBA can analyze the progress or lack of progress. *Remember it is stated in our code of ethics that decisions on programming should only made based upon data.* In applied behavior analysis, we record and graph data to compare performance across baseline and intervention and to determine the effectiveness of the intervention. In addition, if we determine that the intervention is not effective, we modify the intervention based upon an analysis of the data using visual inspection (i.e. we evaluate the data in graphical format to see the effects of the intervention). *As an RBT, one of your responsibilities will be to maintain the data and graph so that the BCBA or BCaBA can analyze the data or behavior.*

Before we go into how to create graphs that represent your data, let's talk about what a graph is and should include. A graph visually represents the occurrences of a behavior over time. The basic elements of a graph include: the x- and y-axis, axis labels, units for x and y, data points, data paths, phase change lines, phase labels, and a brief descriptive label for the graph. When you record data, you will be recording the behavior and some measure of time (i.e., days, session number, etc.). The y-axis (the vertical axis) represents occurrences of the behavior, and the x-axis (the horizontal axis) represents time (usually expressed in days, dates, or sessions).

There are three basic graph formats used within behavior analysis: line graph, bar graph, and standard celeration chart. When graphing your data, you can use a pencil and paper or a computer assisted program. Given the need for electronic formats to be included in reports to funding sources, we will focus on using MicroSoft Excel®.

In a line graph, you are entering data (the y-axis) from each session (x-axis) and the data point will represent the intersection of x and y. The first step in creating a graph is to open the Excel program and then select which kind of graph you want to make. Let's make a line graph.

Step 1: Open the program and enter the data into a workbook.

Sessions	BL	TX
1	10	#N/A
2	13	#N/A
3	11	#N/A
4	9	#N/A
5	#N/A	35
6	#N/A	40
7	#N/A	46
8	#N/A	54
9	#N/A	55
10	#N/A	56

Step 2: Highlight the data you want to graph.

Sessions	BL	TX
1	10	#N/A
2	13	#N/A
3	11	#N/A
4	9	#N/A
5	#N/A	35
6	#N/A	40
7	#N/A	46
8	#N/A	54
9	#N/A	55
10	#N/A	56

Step 3: Select the "Line Graph" tab, and select "Marked Line."

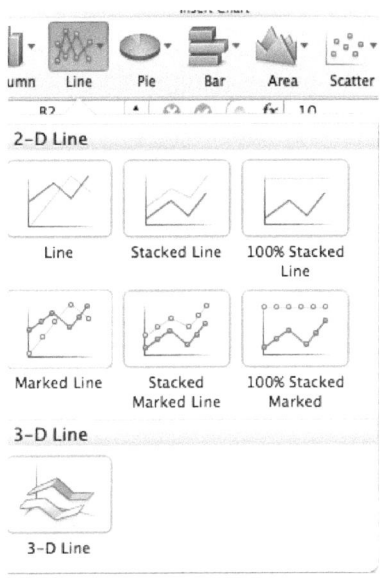

Step 4: Click on the graph until it is highlighted. Then, clink on the "Chart Layout" tab at the top.

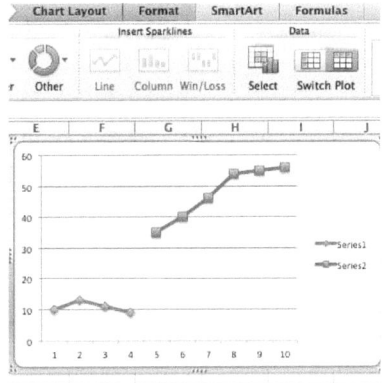

Step 5: Under "Chart Layout," go into the following tabs and "fix" your graph. Under "Axis Titles," select "Horizontal Axis Title," and then select "Axis Below." This is where you enter your time measurement. In this example enter, "Sessions." Go back into "Axis Titles," select "Vertical Axis Title," and then select "Rotated Title." This is where you enter your measurement system. For this example enter "Frequency of Aggression." Next, go to the "Legend Tab" and select "no legend". Then, go to the "Gridlines" tab, select "Horizontal Gridlines, and "no gridlines." Your graph should look like this:

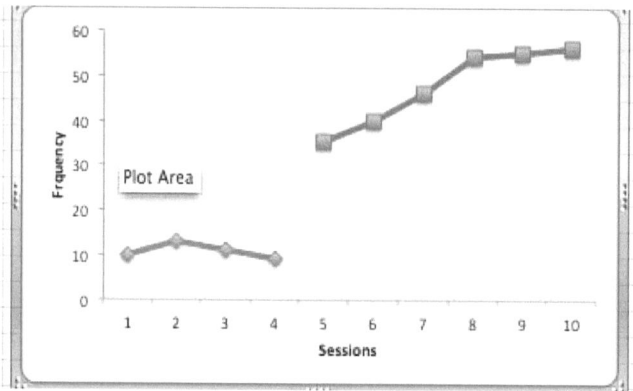

Step 6: Select graph until highlighted, go to "Insert tab" at the top, select "picture," and then "shape." A box of shapes will appear. Select the line. You will then get a + for your cursor. Put cursor + on the x-axis between baseline and treatment (sessions 4 and 5 in this example). Hold the shift key, and draw your line up.

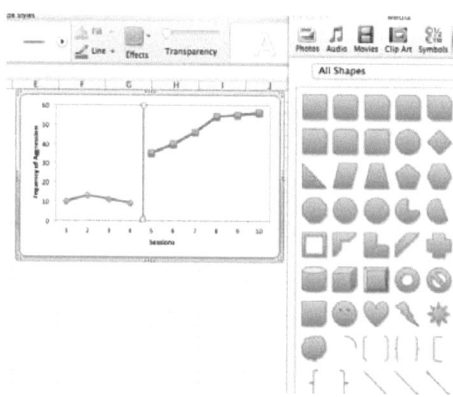

Step 7: Given that the data in the treatment is the same behavior as in baseline, we need to make the data points and the connecting line the same in baseline and treatment. Start off by double clicking on one of the data points in the treatment path. A box labeled "Format Data Series" will pop up. Select the "Marker Style," and then select the matching marker from baseline.

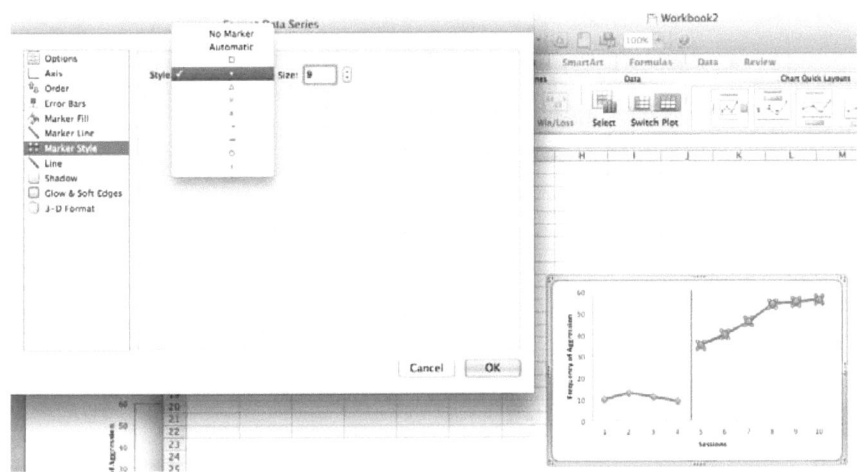

Step 8: Now change the other aspects of the marker and the line by systematically changing them to match baseline.

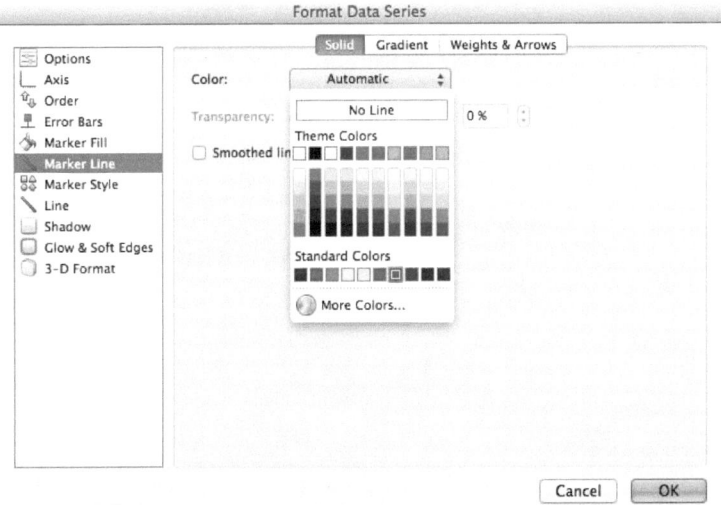

54 • CHAPTER 5

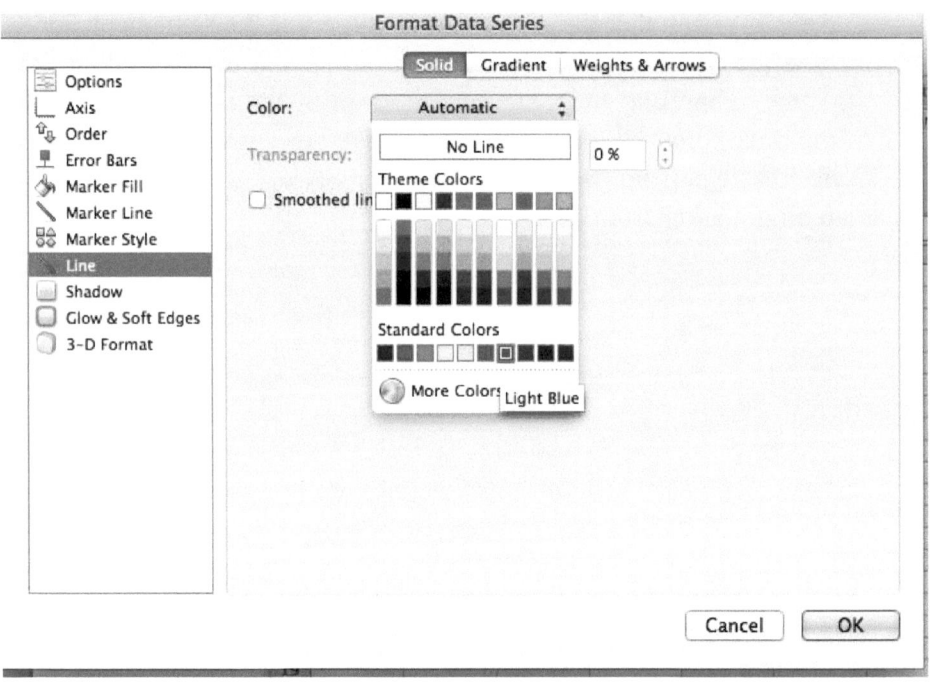

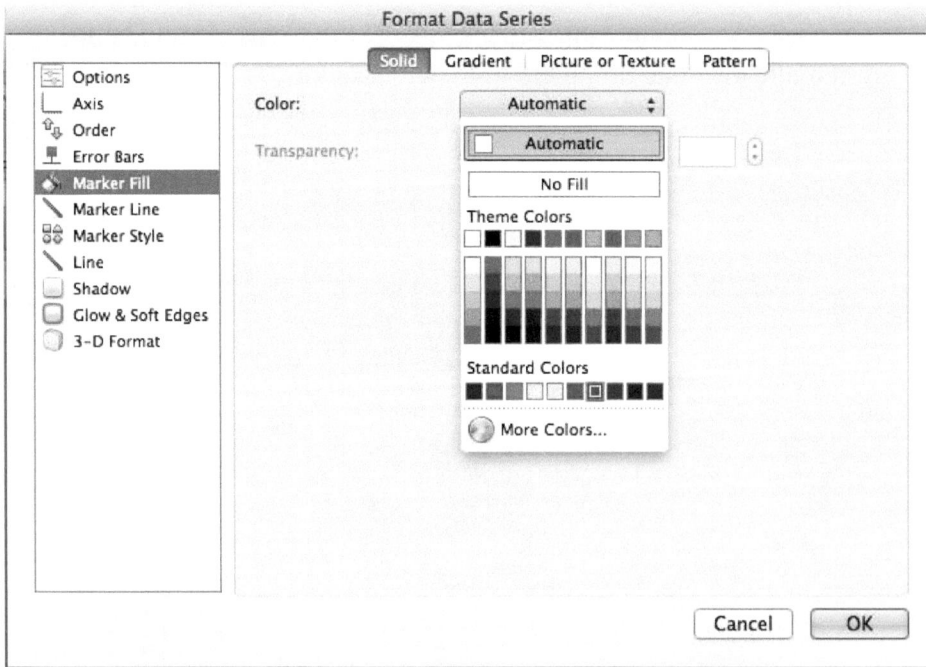

After you have changed the marker and line, your graph should look like this:

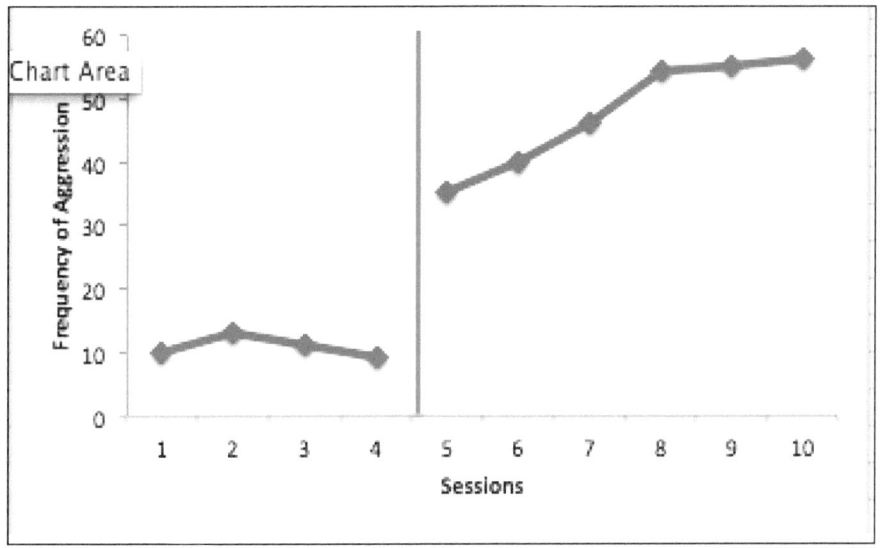

Step 9: Now, highlight the graph, and copy and paste it into a word document. Insert a text box over baseline, and label it "baseline." Insert a text box over treatment, and label it "treatment." Insert a text box with client's name. Your graph should look like this.

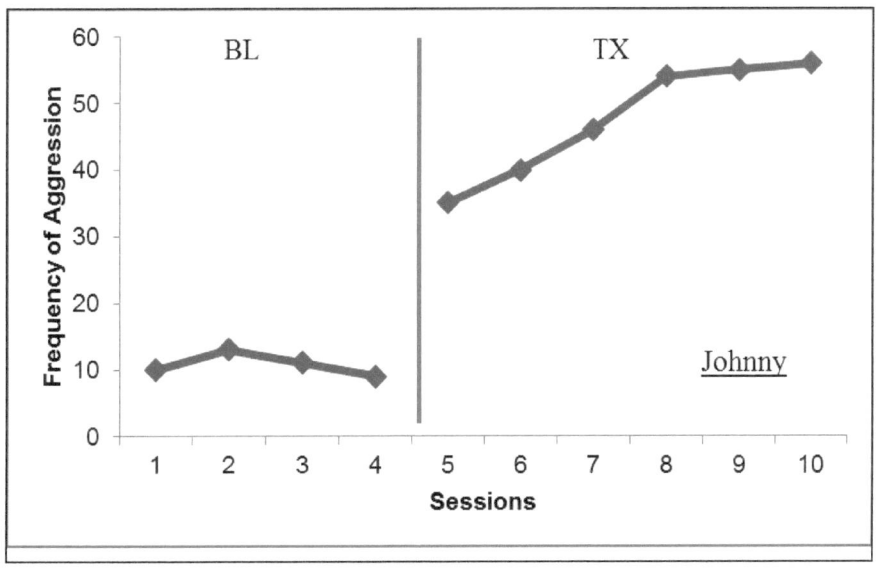

We should mention that in the above example, we were measuring one behavior under one condition. If you are measuring more than one behavior or more conditions, you will have multiple data series and will need to label them either using a legend or a text box.

It is also possible to graph directly in MicroSoft Word®. For a bar graph, you would select "Column," and then "Cluster" (basically, follow the same procedures as above from here). Generally, line graphs are used if the data points are the same behavior. However, a bar graph is utilized when the data points are not the same. The main difference between line and bar graphs is that a bar graph may depict a variety of unrelated responses without sequential order, but a line graph measures the continuing chain of related responses. For example, you would use a bar graph to measure number of minutes played with various toys with the different toys listed on the x-axis instead of time. You can use a bar graph when you want to report grouped data, such as: the monthly frequency of aggression, self-injurious behavior (SIB), and disruption across months where months would be on the x-axis.

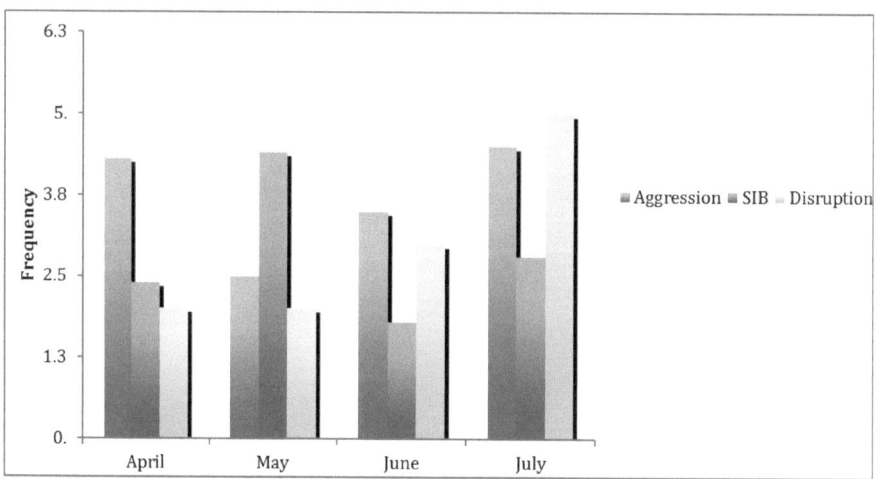

A Standard Celeration Chart (SCC) is for plotting rate of performance. It is generally used to measure fluency of performance (e.g., how fast and accurate behavior can be expressed). An SCC measures the personal progress of each behavior by focusing on the percent the behavior improved. Thus, the behaviors are compared by independent improvements in performance rather than the number of occurrences. Here is a screen shot of a Standard Celeration Chart.

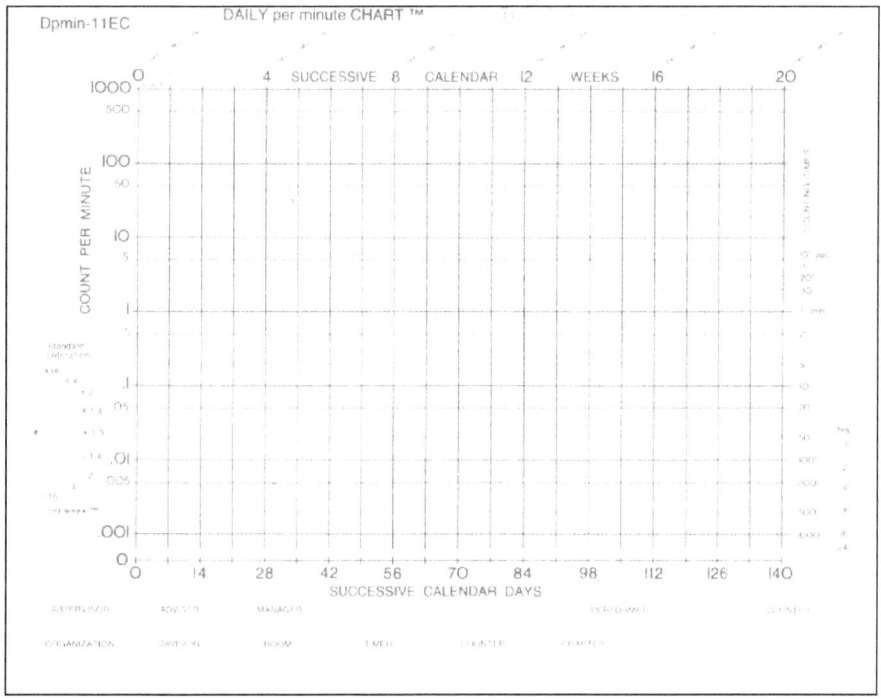

With a SCC, it is important to note that every day has a vertical line and that the y-axis is based upon rate per minute. When graphing on this graph, you would go to the day to plot the rate per minute of performance for that date. For a more detailed tutorial, we urge you to go to

www.behaviorresearchcompany.com/index.php?main_page=page_2

to view the "Charting Rates with Stephanie Bates" module. If your agency uses SSC, they will have to provide you with either physical copies of the chart or a program that allows you to chart.

SCC charting is very helpful when you not only want to look at frequency or duration of a behavior, but how rapidly or fluently the behavior occurs as well. For example, two clients may both score 100% on a test. However, one completes it in 20 minutes, while the other takes an hour to complete it. Which knows the material better? SCC will show this difference between your clients. Thus, it can be most helpful when teaching fluency of a skill.

SCC takes considerable training and time to learn how to do, which is beyond the scope of this book. The tutorial page listed above can help, but supervised instruction and feedback are usually needed to learn this type of graphing.

SUMMARY AND CONCLUSIONS

In ABA, we make decisions on behavior and programming by analyzing data. To ensure you are taking valid and reliable data, report interobsever agreement for at least 33% of observation sessions. The most common way to report data is by depicting performance in one of three types of graphs: line, bar, or SCC; however, the line graph is the graph most often used in depicting ABA data. By inserting the data into a computer program, you can select the type of graph you want to develop. There are a number of steps involved in creating graphs. It is wise to practice and/or make templates that you can insert your data into for graphing purposes. If you choose to use an SCC, you will likely be charting by way of paper and pencil.

EXERCISES

After you have completed the exercises below, you will want feedback. Your instructor has access (or can obtain access from the publisher) to sample answers for each of the following exercises:

1. Describe the advantages of having two observers who simultaneously record identical episodes of the same behavior.
2. What is the most common type of graph used in ABA reports of client progress?
3. Why do you usually need to allow for adaptation before collecting baseline data?
4. How do you know when to terminate (a) the adaption phase and (b) the baseline phase?

5. Robbie has a difficult time remaining on task. You have been asked to collect baseline date on the longest amount of time he remains on task (i.e., working on his math) between prompts (e.g., Robbie, please do your work), and the number of prompts given during the math session, each of three days during the week, both at school and home. You begin collecting data for your baseline and notice that he frequently looks at you, asks his mother and teacher why you are here, etc. Can you use the data you are collecting for baseline data? Why?

ACTIVITIES

1. Select a behavior that you or a friend would like to occur. This can be a behavior of yours or your friends that does not occur as frequently as desired, or does not occur at all but it is one you believe can occur. It might replace a behavior that you do not want to engage in. Operationalize it. Select an appropriate observational method. Record its occurrence independently but simultaneously with a friend, a fellow student, or supervisor. Calculate the reliability of your observation. Discuss between the two of you how you might improve the reliability you obtained.

2. Find a video on You Tube of someone engaging in a behavior. Develop a measurement system and then have a friend use the measurement system to record the behavior on the video while you record the same behavior, and then compare your recordings.

Chapter 6

ABCs of Assessment

GOALS

1. Describe why assessment is important in behavior analysis.
2. What is utilized in determining contingencies?
3. What are the three components of a Functional Behavior Assessment?
4. Why is conducting an FBA important before developing an intervention for problem behavior?
5. Define what is meant by functional vs. arbitrary reinforcers.
6. What methods are used to identify reinforcers for individuals in behavior analysis?
7. Differentiate among single stimulus assessment, paired stimulus assessment, multiple-stimulus assessment with or without replacement, and free operant assessments for identifying highly effective reinforcers.
8. Describe some environmental variables that can influence the effectiveness of items identified in a

preference assessment with respect to reinforcement effects.

9. Describe how the concepts of indirect, descriptive, and functional analyses relate to assessing adaptive behavior.
10. Complete this chapter's exercises/activities, or those assigned by your instructor.

*****

In the last couple of chapters we have talked about how to measure and report data on behavior. You may be saying that it seems like a lot of work to record data and report data on the behaviors my client does or does not emit. You may be thinking, what's the purpose? The purpose of collecting reliable and valid data on behavior and reporting it is so we can predict and control the emission of the behavior. In other words, it is so we can use behavior analysis procedures to teach or increase behavior we want our clients to emit, and we use it to eliminate or teach them not to engage in behavior we don't want them to do. However, collecting the data in and of itself is not good enough. We have to analyze behavior (that is, find trends in behavior through calculated and graphed data; see Chapter 5) so that we can make appropriate intervention changes. We know that if a person is engaging in a behavior we don't want them to do, they are getting reinforced for doing so (they would not engage in the behavior if they were not receiving reinforcement). Thus, the first step in trying to eliminate behavior we don't want to see is to look at under what conditions the behavior occurs [the antecedents (A)], and what reinforces the behavior [the consequences (C)]. Taken together, we need to analyze the A-B-Cs associated with that behavior. By analyzing ABC data correctly, the function (or true purpose) behind the behavior will be revealed. Thus, graphed data can show us why your client takes part in the behavior and what is gained from engaging in the behavior. Likewise, if the person is not engaging in a behavior that we want them to do, we know that the ABCs are not promoting or reinforcing that behavior. Thus, we must identify how to correct the situation.

We have addressed different antecedent strategies to utilize during skill acquisition programs as well as reinforcement-based programs. However, we have not yet taught you how to identify possible reinforcers. Thus, the purpose of this chapter is to teach you how to assess the environment to identify contingencies that are maintaining problematic behavior, and how to identify possible reinforcers to utilize in both skill acquisition as well as behavior reduction programs.

ABCs of Problem Behavior

We know that a behavior occurs if it is either being reinforced by social-positive (e.g., attention, access to tangibles), social-negative (e.g., successfully escaping a demand or postponing an aversive event), or automatic reinforcement (e.g., sensory stimulation or elimination). When trying to figure out why someone engages in a particular behavior, we need to identify the reinforcement contingency that is maintaining it. To do so, we must conduct indirect and direct assessments and analyses of the ABCs. This process of trying to identify the maintaining variables of a problem behavior is called a Functional Behavior Assessment (FBA). An FBA generally consists of an Indirect Assessment, Descriptive Assessment, and Functional Analysis.

Indirect assessments try to identify the *A*s and *C*s that typically occur with the behavior of interest. This is accomplished by asking individuals, who have witnessed the client engaging in the behavior, to remember the environmental variables surrounding the behavior. There are both standardized as well as organization-specific examples of indirect assessments. As an RBT, you might be asked to conduct such assessments with parents, teachers, or other caregivers. The important thing to remember is to try and be neutral when you conduct these assessments to eliminate any biases you may have that could influence your evaluation of certain *A*s and *C*s on the behavior. It is important to understand that indirect assessments are only the first step in a complete FBA.

Descriptive Assessments are used to record the *A*s and *C*s by direct observation that co-occur with the behavior of interest. You are watching and recording first-hands accounts of what is occurring in the natural environment right before the behavior (*A*s), and how the environment reacts in response to the behavior (*C*s). It is not uncommon for RBTs to be responsible for conducting descriptive assessments. While conducting a descriptive assessment, it is important to record objective information as the behavior is occurring. For example, you observed that when Kay asked her mom for a popsicle, her mom said, "No, not till after dinner." When Kay started tantruming in response, her mom gave her the popsicle and said, "fine." You must record the ABCs immediately, and not an hour later when your recall could be affected. Thus, you would immediately record: A = Kay asked for popsicle and mom said no; B = Kay started tantruming; and C = mom gave her the popsicle. After you have collected enough examples of the ABCs surrounding the behavior, the BCBA will analyze them to determine which contingency (social positive, social negative, or automatic) is responsible for maintaining the problem behavior.

We should note that correlation does not mean causation, and in behavior analysis we seek causation. Thus, the next step in trying to understand why an individual engages in problem behavior is to test suspecting variables to see if they are responsible for turning behavior on or off. This is accomplished in a *functional analysis*. The role of the RBT in a functional analysis is to help the BCBA conduct the conditions and/or record data during the various conditions. Regarding the above example with Kay, a BCBA with your help might arrange for two conditions: a) tangible condition where Kay is denied access to the popsicle and is given a small amount contingent on her engaging in the tantrum behavior; and b) control condition where Kay is given free access to popsicles. These conditions would be conducted multiple times, while you record the occurrence of the target behavior (tantruming in this case). After completion of a number of sessions, the BCBA would take the data you recorded on the occurrence of tantrums during these two sessions and analyze if there is a reinforcement effect during the tangible condition (meaning, does Kay engage in tantruming more when it is delivered contingent on her engaging in tantruming than when it is not delivered contingent on tantruming). The information that is gathered from the FBA is what the BCBA will utilize to develop the intervention that you will implement to decrease problem behavior. Thus, your assessment of the ABCs will be extremely important in determining the course of intervention for your client. With that said, given the nature of the assessment and that it has the potential to increase problem behavior (be it temporarily), you should *never* conduct an FBA without direct supervision.

Identifying Functional Reinforcers

Completion of an FBA will lead to the identification of the A and Cs controlling the problem behavior (B), which can then be manipulated in various behavior reduction programs (see Chapters 10 & 11 for more details). When the reinforcement contingency is identified in an FBA, it is said that the **functional** reinforcer was identified. The functional reinforcer can be utilized to reinforce an alternative replacement behavior that is equally as reinforcing and more socially acceptable. However, there are occasions when the functional reinforcer cannot, or should not, be used in behavior reduction interventions. Sometimes, when trying to teach or promote a new behavior, one must add additional reinforcers if the functional reinforcer is not motivating enough to get the person to engage in the behavior. This type of reinforcer is called an **arbitrary** reinforcer, because it is not what naturally reinforces the behavior in the person's everyday life. For example, if we wanted to get Andy to play with Bill, the functional reinforcer would be the social interaction Andy gets from playing with Bill. However, social interaction is not a reinforcer for Andy. In this case, we are going to have to use arbitrary reinforcers to get Andy playing with Bill. This probably all seems logical, but you might be wondering what to use as a reinforcer to get Andy to play with Bill. Then, you remember you really like _____ (insert your favorite item here), so why not use it. Well, we hate to tell you this, but Andy doesn't like _____. Therefore, using it will not increase Andy's playing with Bill. What are you to do?

Identifying Arbitrary Reinforcers

That's right, you have to assess and observe the environment, and identify what is reinforcing for Andy. Just like identifying the functional reinforcer for problem behavior, we use similar assessment strategies to identify arbitrary reinforcers. That is, we use both indirect and direct methods of assessment.

Indirect assessments consist of identifying what someone likes or dislikes by asking them or their parents, caregivers, teachers, friends, etc. As when identifying functional reinforcers, it is not okay to solely rely on indirect assessments when identifying arbitrary ones. With that said, it is likely that you will need to conduct indirect assessments to identify potential arbitrary reinforcers to use within your client's programs. There are a number of free online examples that you could use, or you could simply ask what the client likes in a number of different categories (e.g., snacks, activities, toys, videos, drinks, etc.). Remember though, this is done just to give you an idea of what kinds of arbitrary reinforcers you will assess utilizing a direct assessment method.

In **direct** assessment methodologies, the focus is on directly observing the individual in their natural environment (**descriptive**) to see what they gravitate toward or to conduct an explicit assessment wherein you provide choices and record what the individual selects (**Preference Assessment**).

When conducting a descriptive assessment to identify arbitrary reinforcers, you basically ensure that the items you identified from the indirect assessment are available, and you record which items the individual consumes or interacts with. You include in your recordings how much they consume or interact with the item and create a hierarchy of items from most-to-least interaction. Thus, you can conclude that the top items are likely to be more reinforcing than the lower items. Besides just observing what the client selects, you can actually conduct a formal assessment. It is best to conduct frequent preference assessments, because an item's reinforcing value will likely change over time.

There are a number of formats one can utilize to conduct a preference assessment: Single-stimulus, Paired-stimulus, Multiple-stimulus with replacement, Multiple-stimulus without replacement, and a Free-operant format. In a **Single-Stimulus Assessment**, you present a single item to individuals and record whether or not they consume the item (e.g., eat, drink, interact). You "test" the items (for the value they place on each hypothetical reinforcer) from your indirect assessment, individually. Summarize your results with respect to which items they choose vs. which items they did not choose, and how much time they spent with the non-edible items.

Similarly in a **Paired-Stimulus Assessment**, you present pairs of stimuli to individuals and record which stimulus the individual chooses. Make sure to pair each stimulus with every other stimulus. This will reveal how the reinforcing values of the items you found in your indirect assessment compare to one another. Next, report the percentage of times the individual choses the item by dividing the number of times they selected it by the number of times it was presented (see Paired Stimulus Preference Assessment form). After you complete the assessment, you would graph the percentage of times chosen in a bar graph.

In a **Multiple-Stimulus Assessment with or without Replacement**, you present an array of items to each individual and ask them to pick one. In the one with replacement, you would replace the item chosen in the array on the next trial. In the one without replacement, you do not replace the item and present the remaining items on the next trial. In the end, after you have presented all the trials (which should be equal to the number of items being tested), you calculate preference in two ways: (1) by dividing 1 by the trial number it was chosen for without replacement, or (2) the number of times chosen by the trials number for each item with replacement. Another way to identify reinforcers is by conducting a **Free-Operant Assessment**, in which you place a number of items out and let the individuals interact with them. You record the amount of times they interact with each item and divided it by the observation time. For a sample listing of consequences often found to operate effectively as reinforcers, see the page labeled "Illustrative Reinforcers" on this book's website.

If you would like to watch a model of how to conduct these various preference assessments either shadow your supervisor or watch one of the various available video models on YouTube. For example, you can search "multiple stimulus without replacement preference assessment" on YouTube and will be able to view multiple-stimulus assessments without replacement for both food as well as tangible items. Like all procedures presented in this text, it is advised that you illustrate competency with your supervisor prior to implementing them independently.

Other Important Environmental Variables Affecting Reinforcer Effectiveness

One thing to remember when you conduct these assessments is that other environmental variables will affect how well these items actually reinforce and maintain behavior. One main variable to think about is how much access the person has to the particular item outside of your sessions. If they have free access to the item outside of session, that item may not reinforce performance during session. For example, one of the authors *loves* chocolate, so chocolate would typically be highly preferred. However, if I just ate a box of chocolate, and you are now trying to use chocolate to get me to perform, guess what? Yep, I'm not going to perform (chances are I will be in a chocolate induced coma resting in my bed). So, it is important not only to assess the preference for items, but also to assess how accessible the items are. One suggestion is to limit access to the items you have identified in your preference assessment to increase the individual's motivation to engage in behavior to obtain those items.

Another thing to remember is quality does matter. For example, if you used expensive chocolate in the preference assessment and try to use cheap chocolate in my programming, I will not work for cheap chocolate. Finally, it is also important to remember that preferences can change over time, so it is important to repeat these assessments on a regular basis. Some RBTs even take the top items from the assessment and present a mini-paired choice assessment before a session. For example, do you want to work for item A or item B?

How you deliver the reinforcers also is important. Be sure to deliver the reinforcer(s) *immediately* following the behavior, and *specify the behavior* you want to reinforce when teaching or increasing a behavior. Immediate reinforcement and specifying the behavior fosters discrimination learning, while delayed reinforcement often results in a behavior other than the intervening behavior getting reinforced. Not specifying the behavior you are reinforcing can result in confusion by the client as to what occurred that earned the reinforcer. Also, deliver the reinforcers following each time the behavior occurs, or as often as feasible. The more frequently the behavior is reinforced, the more quickly it will become established. After the target behavior becomes established it is time to begin to: (a) teach delay of gratification, and (b) thin out your frequency of reinforcer delivery.

Preference Assessment Forms

Paired Stimulus Assessment Form

Name_____ Date_____

I. Identify 7 items you would like to test and list below:

Item 1: _____ Item 2: _____
Item 3: _____ Item 4: _____
Item 5: _____ Item 6: _____
Item 7: _____

II. After you have gathered the items, pair each item with every other item and circle the item they select. When you present the items, state "Pick the one you want." If they attempt to grab both, block and represent the command to pick one. After they have selected one, allow them a brief time to consume the item (i.e., 30 sec to 1 min for leisure items and a small piece or amount if it is a food or drink) and then present the next pair.

Item pairing:

1 x 7	6 x 3	4 x 5	1 x 5	2 x 7
4 x 6	5 x 2	6 x 7	2 x 1	5 x 3
7 x 4	3 x 1	5 x 7	7 x 3	4 x 1
3 x 4	6 x 2	1 x 6	2 x 3	6 x 5
4 x 2				

III. Calculating Percentage Selected:
  Item 1: # Selected/ 6 = _____
  Item 2: # Selected/ 6 = _____
  Item 3: # Selected/ 6 = _____
  Item 4: # Selected/ 6 = _____
  Item 5: # Selected/ 6 = _____
  Item 6: # Selected/ 6 = _____
  Item 7: # Selected/ 6 = _____

Multiple-Stimulus W/O Relacement Assessment Form

Name_____ Date_____

I. Identify 7 items you would like to test and list below:

Item 1: _____   Item 2: _____
Item 3: _____   Item 4: _____
Item 5: _____   Item 6: _____
Item 7: _____

II. After you have gathered the items, present the items according to the trials below and state "Pick the one you want." If they attempt to grab more than one item, block and represent the command to pick one. After they have selected one, allow them a brief time to consume the item (i.e., 30 sec to 1 min for leisure items and a small piece or amount if it is a food or drink), circle the item selected AND block that item number out of remaining trials, and then move on to the next trial.

TRIAL 1: 1 x 2 x 3 x 4 x 5 x 6 x 7

TRIAL 2: 1 x 2 x 3 x 4 x 5 x 6 x 7

TRIAL 3: 1 x 2 x 3 x 4 x 5 x 6 x 7

TRIAL 4: 1 x 2 x 3 x 4 x 5 x 6 x 7

TRIAL 5: 1 x 2 x 3 x 4 x 5 x 6 x 7

TRIAL 6: 1 x 2 x 3 x 4 x 5 x 6 x 7

TRIAL 7: 1 x 2 x 3 x 4 x 5 x 6 x 7

III. Calculating Percentage Selected

Item 1: 1/Trial Selected _____   Item 2: 1/Trial Selected _____

Item 3: 1/Trial Selected _____   Item 4: 1/Trial Selected _____

Item 5: 1/Trial Selected _____   Item 6: 1/Trial Selected _____

Item 7: 1/Trial Selected _____

Multiple-Stimulus with Relacement Assessment Form

Name_____ Date_____

I. Identify 7 items you would like to test and list below:

Item 1: _____   Item 2: _____
Item 3: _____   Item 4: _____
Item 5: _____   Item 6: _____
Item 7: _____

II. After you have gathered the items, present the items according to the trials below and state "Pick the one you want." If they attempt to grab more than one item, block and represent the command to pick one. After they have selected one, allow them a brief time to consume the item (i.e., 30 sec to 1 min for leisure items and a small piece or amount if it is a food or drink), circle the item selected, and then move on to the next trial.

TRIAL 1: 1 x 2 x 3 x 4 x 5 x 6 x 7

TRIAL 2: 1 x 2 x 3 x 4 x 5 x 6 x 7

TRIAL 3: 1 x 2 x 3 x 4 x 5 x 6 x 7

TRIAL 4: 1 x 2 x 3 x 4 x 5 x 6 x 7

TRIAL 5: 1 x 2 x 3 x 4 x 5 x 6 x 7

TRIAL 6: 1 x 2 x 3 x 4 x 5 x 6 x 7

TRIAL 7: 1 x 2 x 3 x 4 x 5 x 6 x 7

III. Calculating Percentage Selected

Item 1: # Selected/7 = _____   Item 2: # Selected/7 = _____

Item 3: # Selected/7 = _____   Item 4: # Selected/7 = _____

Item 5: # Selected/7 = _____   Item 6: # Selected/7 = _____

Item 7: # Selected/7 = _____

Skill Assessment

You guessed it: before we can leave assessment strategies we need to see how they are applied to get an idea of what skills someone can and cannot do. Again, there are three main types of skill assessments: indirect, descriptive, and functional analyses. With indirect assessments you can ask caregivers about the ability of the client (e.g., The Vineland Adaptive Behavior Scale). This approach is a common approach used by medical doctors. When you take a child for a check up, the doctor has you fill out a sheet of paper that asks if your child can perform certain milestones. Descriptive assessment asks that you observe the client and record whether or not they can perform some skill. Some assessments will ask you to give your child a pen and see if he can draw a line rather than just if you think he can or not. Generally, functional analyses are restricted to individuals with severe or persistent behavior issues. For example, an occupational therapist might present a spoon to a child's mouth and record if the child places her tongue in the correct spot upon insertion. Or, a BCBA might use a functional assessment to determine if a child can tact common household items by presenting the item and asking "What is it?" and recording if the child can correctly tact the items. In behavior analysis it is important that we assess someone's skills before we embark on the journey to teach them.

With respect to formal skill assessments, there are a number of great ones that have been developed over the last decade (we will let your supervising BCBAs formally train you on the one they use). The main thing they all have in common is that they take a curriculum and test for skills by presenting the S^D related to the skill and recording if the behavior occurs or not. For example, if testing for addition skills, the child might be asked, "What is 2 + 3:, 5 + 5; etc." to determine what additions skills the child can perform and cannot perform.

SUMMARY AND CONCLUSIONS

This chapter highlights the importance of assessment when you want to decrease an unwanted behavior or increase a desirable behavior, by identifying current maintaining contingencies and potential reinforcers, respectfully. When trying to identify the maintaining reinforcer(s) for a specific aberrant behavior, it is important to conduct a Functional Behavioral Assessment including an indirect assessment (gathering information by indirect measures), a descriptive assessment (recording and identifying contingencies in the natural context) and a functional analysis (manipulating contingencies to test if they are actually supporting the behavior). Moreover, when trying to increase a behavior, it is important to have powerful reinforcers connected to the behavior of interest. These reinforcers can be those identified to maintain problem behavior and/or can be arbitrary reinforcers identified within a preference assessment. An important step in ensuring an item is a reinforcer is to conduct a preference assessment. This can be accomplished by conducting a single-stimulus, paired-stimulus, multiple-stimulus, or a free-operant assessment. Finally, regardless of methodology used to select a reinforce, it is important to assess the availability of the item outside of session (less available = more effective), the quality of the item (higher quality = more effective), and provide the reinforcers frequently and immediately following the behavior you are teaching. Approaching skill acquisition from an assessment standpoint is a well thought-out plan. So before assuming individuals can or can't do something, ask, watch, and test whether they can or can't.

EXERCISES

After you have completed the exercises below, you will want feedback. Your instructor has access (or can obtain access from the publisher) to sample answers for each of the following exercises:

1. Based on the following A-B-C analyses, what is the probable function for (a) Ramon's tantrum and (b) the mother giving him the toy?

A	B	C
Mother says "no" when Ramon requests toy at store.	Ramon screams, hits, and runs.	Mother gives Ramon toy to settle him down.
Ramon screams, hits, and runs.	Mother gives him the toy.	Ramon becomes quiet. Mother experiences relief.

2. Based on the following A-B-C analyses, what is the probable function for (a) Sally's tantrum and (b) for the mother talking to her?

A	B	C
Sally tells mother that she is hungry. Mother informs her that she is busy and that she will have to fix something for herself.	Sally runs around the house throwing books off book cases, knocking over chairs, etc.	Mother pulls Sally aside and quietly talks to her about what they can do together at a later time.
Sally's tantrum.	Mother talks to her and makes plans to do something together.	Sally stops the tantrum.

3. Based on the following A-B-C analyses, what is the probable function for Tyrone's aggressive behavior and the teacher's allowing him to do what he wants to do?

A	B	C
Tyrone is aggressive.	Mother allows him to do what he wants.	Tyrone stops his aggression.
Told to put away what he is working on. Asked to allow others a turn. Told he cannot do what he wants to do.	Tyrone swears, hits, and/or threatens others.	He is often allowed to do what he wants to do.

4. Sue's mother, teacher and Sue are asked what her high preference activities are. Is this a preference assessment?

ACTIVITIES

1. Go to a public location and try and conduct an A-B-C analysis of someone's behavior. Specify the purpose or function of the behavior from your A-B-C analysis.
2. Do an indirect assessment for possible reinforcers by interviewing your friend and/or yourself.

3. Conduct four types of preference assessments with a friend and/or yourself. Compare the results with your indirect assessment. Which preference assessment do you prefer conducting and why?
4. Develop a step-by-step skill assessment for an adaptive behavior.

Chapter 7
Skill Acquisition

GOALS

1. Define:
    a. Discrimination training
    b. Target behavior
    c. DTT
    d. Incidental teaching
    e. Shaping
    f. Chaining, including forward chaining, backward chaining and the whole, concurrent, or total task methods
    g. Task analysis
    h. Verbal behavior

2. Describe and illustrate how to use discrimination training with a client's behavior.

3. Give an example, not already provided in this chapter, of highlighting critical elements to promote discrimination.

4. Illustrate using DTT with flash cards.
5. Illustrate how to use incidental teaching with addition.
6. Illustrate the use of backward chaining with using the phone.
7. Describe how chaining can help us teach various social skills.
8. Give an example of the following verbal behavior terms:
   a. Mands
   b. Tacts
   c. Duplic behavior and its three types
   d. Intraverbals
9. Complete this chapter's exercises/activities or those assigned by your instructor.

*****

A large part of behavioral services are geared toward developing and teaching new skills and overcoming behavioral deficits. This chapter covers basic skill acquisition methodology that you will use when providing behavioral services. In addition, we have provided a brief overview of one of the most important skill deficits faced by behavior therapists, *verbal behavior*, or teaching someone how to communicate.

USING DISCRIMINATION TRAINING PROGRAMS

Discrimination training involves *teaching your client to know under what conditions a behavior is likely to be reinforced or not reinforced.* This restricts the variety of S^Ds that evoke the response. The major teaching tool that you use to teach discrimination is differential reinforcement. That is, you reinforce the behavior only under certain conditions or set of stimuli, and you do not reinforce it under other conditions or stimuli. For example, you reinforce the client saying the word "red" only in the presence of the color red and not under other conditions, such as in the presence of yellow, black, etc. You reinforce the answer 6 to the problem 3 x 2, not other answers such as 5 or 9.

There are a number of things you can do to help your client make appropriate discriminations:

- Specify the features of the behavior to be reinforced. Specifying and modeling (e.g., demonstrating) the behavior (described in Chapters 8 and 10) often helps clients identify the behavior's features, or what it is you want them to do. For example, when teaching your clients to raise their hand in a classroom, you can show and tell them that the hand goes above the head. When printing letters, you can show them and stress how high the letter "l" goes.
- Specify the conditions under which the reinforcers will be delivered. In other words, help your clients identify in what situations the **target behavior** (i.e., the behavior to which you are applying your interventions) is likely to be reinforced and the situations in which the target behavior will not be reinforced. For example, hand-raising will not be reinforced on the playground but will be in the classroom during discussion time. Or, it is ok to try to talk to mom when she is relaxing, but not when she is on the phone or talking to another person.
- Provide the reinforcers immediately following the target behavior. If you wait to provide the reinforcement, other behaviors may occur and the reinforcement may follow them rather than your target behavior. Immediate reinforcement facilitates discrimination. For example, you are working on listener behavior. You ask your client to hand you the red card that is in front of him next to the blue and yellow card, and he hands it to you. If you do not reinforce right away, he may pick up the other cards before you reinforce the correct answer. Thus, it is important to reinforce the target behavior immediately.
- Apply differential reinforcement each time the target behavior occurs until it is established. In the above example, you don't want to start increasing the number of occurrences of the target behavior for which you deliver a reinforcer until the client has

met some mastery criteria (say, 100 percent correct across three days).

Once a high, steady rate of discrimination occurs:

- Start intermittent delivery of your reinforcers by gradually thinning their delivery. For example, once your client starts to engage in the target behavior more frequently, refrain from reinforcing every occurrence and only reinforce every other occurrence. Continue to steadily increase the ratio of occurrences you are reinforcing until the target behavior is mastered without reinforcement.
- Introduce delay. As mentioned, immediate reinforcement facilitates discriminations. However, in the real world, immediate reinforcement is not always available. Thus, to help your clients learn to delay gratification (and generalize skills), you need to introduce gradually longer delays between their response and the delivery of the reinforcer. For example, in real life they won't be able to access an activity, event, item, or person every time they ask for it. They will have to learn how to tolerate delays.
- Reduce the nature, size and frequency of the reinforcer delivery *gradually* to help them continue to perform the discrimination even when they are not receiving reinforcement frequently.
- Fade your prompts (e.g., the directions, explanations, and modeling) and within stimulus prompts (e.g., placing critical elements of the stimulus in bold, or using a different color or size) that you used to facilitate the discrimination. To master a skill, the client must not rely on prompts, so prompts should be faded to no prompts.

Let's take a school example to illustrate. Ramon frequently speaks out without raising his hand. The teacher wants him to sit quietly and raise his hand when he has a question or comment. She clearly tells him that he needs to raise his hand and quietly wait to be called on whenever he has a question or comment to make. Later, he blurts out an answer to a question. The teacher ignores his blurting out and calls on another student who has his hand up (to serve as a model). The model provides the answer, and the teacher compliments the student for hand-raising. Also, she reminds students that she only calls on those who are sitting quietly with their hands up (extra prompt provided). Ramon gets the message and sits quietly with his hand up. His teacher calls on him soon after his hand goes up. After he has been called on several times soon after his hand went up, the teacher begins to call on one or two others before calling on him again to introduce delay. As the days continue, she does not always call on him, just most of the time (intermittent reinforcement has been introduced). As time progresses, the teacher continues to fade out her reminders for students to raise their hands and sometimes she calls on Ramon immediately. Other times she calls on him after another student or two, and sometimes, she just calls on others. Due to these tactics, Ramon has now learned to raise his hand and participate only when called upon. Through discrimination training, Ramon learned that hand-raising behavior is reinforced in the classroom with teacher attention, and blurting out in the classroom is not reinforced with teacher attention.

Highlight Critical Elements

To facilitate making accurate discriminations it is often useful (at least initially) to highlight the critical differences between the stimuli or make them very different from one another. Then, you gradually fade out the highlighting and supplemental differences (the prompts). For example, when helping your client differentiate between 2 and 7, highlight the curve in the 2 and stress the straight lines in the 7. Also, you could make one number much larger than the other and a different color. As your client begins to correctly discriminate the differences, gradually fade out the size and color differences, and then the highlighting. Continue to fade until they can discriminate accurately without these sorts of prompts. Part of the issue in helping clients discriminate is helping them focus on the relevant stimuli. For example, we had a client who did not discriminate between addition and subtraction problems even though the "+" or "–" sign preceded the math problems. Thus, we started making the "+" sign a large red color and the "–" sign a green color. This helped him to correctly add or subtract. We then gradually faded out the large size for the "+"

sign, followed by the colors as the client continued to correctly add or subtract.

Discrete Trial Training (DTT)

DTT is often used to help a client engage in a particular response in the presence of the RBT. It is a teaching method that systematically evokes and reinforces a response by structuring the presentation of the instruction and supports in routine steps to show the client what behavior will receive reinforcement. A **discrete trial** consists of four or five basic parts:

1. An antecedent that tells the client what to do (e.g., "match," "What's this?" "Point to ___")
2. If necessary, provide a temporary prompt, such as a model, instructions, or physical guidance.
3. The client emits the requested behavior.
4. The behavior is reinforced.
5. You pause before starting the next trial.

In DDT, complex skills are broken down and repetition of the same target behavior is key to skill acquisition. DTT is often conducted at the table and reinforcement is contrived rather than naturalistic.

To illustrate: You hold up the color red and ask, "What color is this?" The client responds, "Red." You say, "Great! That's correct." You then wait a few seconds before asking the next question. You then hold up the color yellow and ask, "What color is this?" The client does not respond. You say, "Yellow" (prompt) and then the client says, "Yellow." You say, "That's right, it is yellow. Good job."

Flash Cards

Flash cards can also be used to help promote skills acquisition. On one side of the flash card it has the word "color" or a math problem that your client is to learn or solve (e.g., 4 + 4). On the back of the cards, each one has the answer (e.g., 8). You present the card and ask for the answer. Be sure to praise correct responding (e.g., "right," "good," "correct," "you're doing great"). You must also correct errors. Though the most effective correction procedure varies among individuals, modeling appears to be the least intrusive, and often the most effective. Here you model the correct response and have the client imitate it. Another bit more aversive error correction procedure is to say, "No, the correct answer is _____." Then, have the student provide the correct answer after hearing it. Usually, just focus on teaching 3 or 4 cards at a time (this number will vary depending on your client's ability with the task) until your client can respond fluently to each of them. Once you begin to introduce other cards, be sure to periodically review those that your client has learned.

Naturalistic/Incidental Teaching

DTT and flash cards involve very specific, controlled training. However, for your client to generalize the behavior to other situations, people, and time of day, it is best to train loosely or use a more naturalistic training program. Incidental teaching trains loosely in naturalistic settings.

Incidental teaching (IT). Incidental teaching *involves capitalizing on natural opportunities that are sometimes planned and sometimes unplanned.* IT is often used to help children begin to communicate verbally by placing children's preferred objects on display and beyond their reach. To obtain any of them, they must first **mand** (e.g., request) for them. Manding is a way for a child to get what they want in a socially acceptable way, and it replaces problem behaviors that previously provided that access. For example, you could give a client paper to draw with, but keep the crayons across the table. Mand training would teach the client to request the crayons, and then naturally reinforce the request by providing access to the crayons in response. As the child learns to mand for the various objects, their presence can be gradually faded (e.g., placed further and further away from the child). This will teach the child to request the objects without seeing them at the same time. You can also teach your client to **tact**, *or label*, various colors. Rather than holding up a color and asking, "What color is this?" you ask what color various items are around the house and outside. For example, you might ask, "What color is that car?" or, "What color is that flower?" Incidental teaching also is good for teaching your client to name, or tact, objects. For example, you can ask your client: "What is that?" "Point to the couch." "Point to the red car." "What is the name of that?" This way, a greater variety of stimuli become S^{Dr}s (see Chapter 3), evoking the proper response in a variety of situations. So, if generalization is a goal, as it is in most cases, do not use just DTT. It is beneficial to combine DTT with incidental teaching and other generalization strategies (see Chapter 9 for a more extensive discussion of generalization).

Sometimes, RBTs have difficulty identifying and conducting a learning trial during incidental teaching, because they are not specified within the task analyzed protocol. One exercise that can be helpful is to practice identifying learning trials in natural environments. For example, look at the picture oon the next page and identify a minimum of 20 learning trials.

Here are some of the targets that we came up with:

1. Do we go up or down the slide? "down"
2. Do we climb up or down the steps? "up"
3. What is this? "slide," "sand," "grass," "tree," "sky," "clouds," "sand."
4. What color? "blue," "gray," "green," "orange," "white."
5. What shape? "circle," "square."
6. Is this solid or stripped? "solid" "stripped"
7. Is the sand hot or cold? "hot." Is the sand rough or smooth? "rough."

USING SHAPING AND CHAINING TO PROMOTE SKILL ACQUISITION

Shaping

Shaping is used to teach new behaviors by *differentially reinforcing successive approximations toward your client's goal* (i.e., using reinforcement and extinction). For example, let's say your goal is to teach your client to draw a straight line. Currently, when asked to draw a straight line, your client draws a very wobbly line. You start differentially reinforcing that wobbly line. Soon, you notice that some of the lines are a bit less wobbly. You then make your reinforcement contingent on the occurrence of the less wobbly lines and stop reinforcing the very wobbly lines. You continue to note that some are straighter then the others. You remain differentially reinforcing those that are straighter and stop reinforcing the wobblier ones that you were previously reinforcing. You continue to differentially reinforce approximations that are successively closer to your goal of drawing a straight line until you achieve your goal of straight lines. You would approach teaching your client to print or write letters and numbers in a similar fashion.

Shaping is often used to teach eye contact. You might start with differentially reinforcing the client's looking toward your feet, then up to your knees, then your mid-section, etc., until you eventually only reinforce eye contact. It is important when using shaping to make sure that you are differentially reinforcing closer approximations and simultaneously placing previous behavior on extinction. For example, once you start reinforcing the client for looking at your mid-section, you should no longer be reinforcing them for looking at your feet or knees. Shaping can be useful for teaching skills that are difficult to prompt. It can also be useful for teaching verbal responses to early learners, or for increasing sustained attention to tasks.

Shaping also is commonly used in combination with other procedures, such as modeling or demonstrating, to teach clients to speak more clearly and/or loudly enough to be heard, and to engage in motor and sport skills, assertive behavior, sharing, waiting, food acceptance, and many other behaviors.

Contact desensitization is based on shaping. With contact desensitization you *differentially reinforce your client's closer and closer approximations toward approaching an object that the client fears or avoids, while your client continues to relax*. For example, the client fears spiders. A spider in a jar is placed at the far end of the room. Over time, it is gradually moved closer to the client, while the client remains relaxed. Due to the non-threatening gradual exposure to the feared object being repeatedly presented with something reinforcing, the object will begin to loose its fear eliciting quality. Thus, your client will no longer strongly fear or avoid the object. Before using contact desensitization, be sure you have been trained in its use.

Have you ever played the game where you tell another if he is getting warmer or hotter as he moves closer to the item he is looking for? That is a form of shaping as well. You can shape where someone stands in your classroom or to pick up an item located near the rear of the room. Just ensure that each time you say "warmer" or "hotter" he is engaging in a closer approximation to the goal behavior. Rather than saying "warmer" or "hotter," you might try giving attention when he moves closer to the item and withholding the attention as he moves in the wrong direction.

How do you determine which approximation to start at?

- The approximation must be in your client's repertoire and resemble the terminal goal.

- The approximation should produce more success than failure.
- It should be a challenge for your client. You want to communicate from the start that the reinforcement is provided for improvement, not status quo. You are not reinforcing a client's compliance for a known task, but you are reinforcing personal advancements with something specifically difficult for the client.
- You can start slightly above their average baseline level and increase the criterion for reinforcement gradually from there.
- For example, if your client remains on task for 5, 7, 3, 4, and 8 minutes, respectively, we would suggest that you start at about 6 minutes. That it is slightly above your client's average performance, and you have evidence that he can achieve that level without too much difficulty.

How do you use shaping effectively?

- Always keep you eye on the goal and be moving toward it.
- Make sure the target behavior and approximations are clearly defined.
- Select a starting approximation, as described above.
- Select step size and duration based on your client's skill level. If your selected step is too large, your client's failure will tell you that you misjudged. If it is too small, your client will quickly attain it, attend to another activity, or appear bored.
- Combine shaping with prompts such as modeling and instructions.
- Combine with fading to fade out the prompts with which you supplemented the shaping.
- Gradually reduce reinforcement of previously reinforced steps.

Chaining

Chaining is used to teach more complex new behavior. **Chaining** *involves linking a sequence of responses, or tasks, to the same terminal reinforcer* (i.e., the end reinforcer). There are three types of chaining: **forward chaining**, **backward chaining** and **total, concurrent**, or **whole task method**.

The first step to using chaining involves doing a **task analysis** to *identify the sequence of responses that make up the chain, or complex behavior.* There are two basic ways to do a task analysis. One is based on your own experience, where you create a list out of what you think are the steps involved in the skill. The second is to systematically observe a learner correctly demonstrating the skill, and write down each task you observe. Whichever one you want to use, be sure to test it out on others before using it with your client. You may find that some tasks need to be added or subtracted, or that the order of steps might change. The complexity and number of steps in a task analysis depend on the learner.

Let's say we want to teach, "getting the mail." The task analysis might look like:

1. Walk to the mailbox.
2. Open the mailbox.
3. Pull out the mail.
4. Close the mailbox.
5. Walk back.
6. Give the mail to mom.

To use *forward chaining* we would first teach the first step (walking to the mailbox) using modeling (maybe physical guidance if necessary) and reinforce each correct occurrence, eventually without prompts. Once that was learned (prompts are not longer necessary), we would add the second step (opening the mailbox). Here your client would learn to walk the mail to the mailbox and open the mailbox when he arrives. We would continue adding one step at a time until all the steps occur easily for the client.

When using *backward chaining*, you start teaching at the end of the chain. You could take your client to the mailbox, get the mail, and close the box. Then, let your client carry it back to the house and give it to mom. Here the client did the last two steps, while you completed the first. Once these steps are mastered, decrease the number of steps you are doing for your client to 3 steps. Have your client close the mailbox, walk back and give the mail to mom. You continue in this fashion until your client has mastered all 6 steps. Backward chaining should not be a new procedure for you. How did you teach your child, or how were you taught, to use the phone? Wasn't the first step something like, "Here, do you want to talk to your grandma?" You get the phone and start talking — which is the last step in the chain of calling grandma. Then, you were asked if you wanted to call grandma, mom would dial or punch in the number for you and you were told to wait until you hear grandma's voice and then say "Hi grandma" when she answered the phone. Next, you might have been permitted to dial the last #, then, say "Hi" when you hear her voice, etc.

If you were using the *total task method*, you might model or explain all six steps and have the client imitate or do all six steps together. Here, the entire chain is being taught at once.

Let's look at a second example of doing a task analysis for completing double-digit multiplication problems:

1. Multiply the 1s times the 1s.
2. Multiply the 1s times the 10s.
3. Leave a place for the zero.
4. Multiply the 10s times the 1s.
5. Multiply the 10s times the 10s.
6. Add the partial products.

In teaching this sequence of behaviors, we found that using forward chaining was not resulting in much progress. Therefore, we switched to backward chaining. This involved teaching step 6 first, then step 5 and 6, then steps 4–6, etc. We first presented a problem like the following:

$$
\begin{array}{r}
23 \\
\times 41 \\
\hline
23 \\
920 \\
\hline
943
\end{array}
$$

All the clients had to do was add the partial products. After the clients showed that they could accurately add the partial products at least 3 times in a row, we presented:

$$\begin{array}{r} 33 \\ \times 22 \\ \hline 66 \\ \mathbf{660} \\ \hline \mathbf{726} \end{array}$$

This time, the clients not only had to add the partial products, but they also had to multiply the 10s times the 1s and the 10s times the 10s prior to adding the partial products (the last step). After three successful tries, we continued to add steps. Next, we had them hold the place for the zero, in addition to the steps they just completed. Finally, they were doing the entire problem correctly. Why did backward chaining work best? One reason is that the most powerful reinforcer (praise and success) is at the end of the chain, so they are able to achieve it more rapidly with backward chaining. We also had a similar experience in teaching a client to tie his shoes. Forward chaining seemed to frustrate him, but he had immediate success as soon as we started to use backward chaining. He even gave us a big smile because he could see that he finished tying his shoe. He soon learned to tie his shoes using backward chaining. So, if forward chaining is not working as desired, be sure to try backward chaining. Or, try backward chaining first, where you start with the final link (e.g., adding partial products).

If we were to use the *total task* method, the entire math problem or shoe tying might be modeled. Then, the client would be asked to imitate the modeled chain.

Once you have completed and tested the task analysis, the *second step* is that you must make sure your clients can do each of the identified tasks. You cannot chain various links together in their proper order if your client does not do each task. (For example you have a client who does not take his seat and start his work when requested. He talks to someone before taking his seat. He has the skill of taking his seat, and doing his work, but does not do so in the proper order (i.e., he does not go directly to his seat when requested. If your client does not have each skill, you will need to teach those tasks that are missing by using shaping, modeling and/or other prompting methods that we discuss in subsequent chapters.

Step 3 is to start with the final link, if feasible, or use the chaining method prescribed by your BCBA.

Step 4 is to prompt the occurrence of response combinations (i.e., combining skills or links) with various discriminative stimuli (e.g., "Now you need to multiply the 10's times, the 1's and the 10's times the 10's, and then add the partial products. OK? Any questions? Do you want me to show you how?").

Step 5 is to make sure you are using effective reinforcers in addition to the reinforcer of success.

Step 6 involves fading out prompts and thinning the reinforcers that you had to use to help your client successfully complete the chain.

Social skills. Chaining also underlies teaching many social skills. For example, let's say you want to teach a client how to strike up a conversation. The chain might involve the following:

1. Saying "hi" or "hello."
2. Introducing self by name.
3. Asking questions about the other person (e.g., name, likes, etc.).
4. Identifying and discussing common interests.
5. Delivering specific compliments during steps 3 and 4.
6. Sharing something about self.

Or, you might want to teach your client how to request help from a teacher when needed. The steps involved in this skill might include:

1. Raising hand.
2. Continuing to work quietly until teacher responds to the raised hand.

3. Once the teacher responds, state what kind of help is needed or the confusion experienced.

By breaking the complex behavior down into its sub-tasks, it makes it easier to teach and learn. Besides using chaining, you also would want to provide role-playing or practice opportunities in which you provide reinforcement for appropriate responding and prompts (e.g., modeling) to help them learn what to say or do. As they become proficient in the skill, you would fade out the prompts.

VERBAL BEHAVIOR

It takes at least a semester-long class to address the concept of verbal behavior as a topic in ABA. Thus, we are only going to provide you with some of the basic terminology in this specialized area. In ABA the term verbal behavior has a special meaning that more closely resembles communicative behavior. We often think of verbal behavior being the act of speaking to others. However, **verbal behavior** in ABA is defined as *affecting the environment through the behavior of some other person or the person herself* (by using self-talk). You can bring about reinforcement and behavior change by talking to others and by talking to yourself. It takes on many forms: English, Spanish, writing, sign-language, pointing, gestures, Braille, hitting, etc. Thus, the term verbal behavior is not synonymous with vocal behavior (i.e., speaking).

There are numerous terms in the specialty area of verbal behavior. These terms are usually based on the purpose or function of the behavior. For example, we discussed mands and tacts above. When someone **mands**, they are requesting (or demanding) what will function as a reinforcer (water, toy, food, activity, etc.). When **tacting**, a stimulus is being named or labeled, as we pointed out above. We do not use the terms expressive and receptive language. Instead, we use **speaker** and **listener** behaviors. They are more precise, observable and function based. For example in tacting, if a child points to a car and says, "Car," they would be behaving as a speaker. However, they would be behaving as a listener if you said, "Hand me the car," and they handed you the car.

There are 3 types of **Duplic behavior** (this refers to duplication or replicating what is being done):

1. **Echoic**, or verbal imitation (e.g., Say dog: The client says, "Dog.").
2. **Physical imitation**, or doing what you see another do.
3. The third type is called **copying text** (e.g., you print your clients' names and each copies their name).

As you get into the field, you will probably pick up several other verbal behavior terms. However, these should get you started as you work with your BCBA to help clients communicate with others more effectively.

Another verbal behavior that is generally taught in programs relying on ABA is to answer questions. Answering questions is a form of verbal behavior called **intraverbal**. For example, if you ask your client to say his phone number, and he responds, "421–345–9798."

SUMMARY AND CONCLUSIONS

Several skill acquisition strategies were presented in this chapter. We first talked about discrimination training to help your clients learn what behaviors in what situations are likely to receive or not receive reinforcement. Several methods were provided that could help clients make appropriate discriminations. This important topic is further elaborated upon in Chapter 9. Discrete trial training and incidental teaching were discussed and compared in relation to helping clients learn when and where to engage in a behavior. In addition, shaping and chaining were presented. Both of these procedures are used to teach new behavior. Shaping is used to teach a task, or element in a chain, while chaining is used for teaching more complex behavior. An understanding of chaining also can help you teach various social skills. Also, we introduced verbal behavior so that you will be familiar with some of the verbal behavior terms used in the field by your BCBA. Verbal behavior is important in that its understanding can help you and your BCBA assist your client to better communicate with others.

EXERCISES

After you have completed the exercises below, you will want feedback. Your instructor has access (or can obtain access from the publisher) to sample answers for each of the following exercises:

1. Identify the discriminative stimulus and response for each of the following:
    a. The dog goes near the door when Jack rattles his car keys.
    b. The baby stops crying when she is held.
    c. Pizza makes my mouth water.
    d. Harold laughs during his favorite television show.

2. Distinguish between shaping and chaining for teaching new behaviors.

3. If the client can do all the links in a chain, why is chaining necessary?

4. Define forward chaining using as an example teaching caregivers at a nursing home to wash their hands carefully.

5. When a child says, "cookie" is it a mand or tact?

6. If generalization is your goal when teaching a skill, would you stress the use of DTT or incidental teaching? Why?

ACTIVITIES

1. Describe how you have used, or could use, incidental teaching.

2. Walk around the block and keep tract of how many different learning trials/targets you could come up with (e.g., different colors).

3. Go to a public place, take a picture, and develop possible targets for incidental teaching in that environment.

4. Pair up with a friend or other RBT and play with him or her and and be silly for five minutes while presenting possible learning trials.

Chapter 8

Antecedent Procedures in Skill Acquisition

GOALS

1. Define goal setting and describe how goal setting can help evoke behavior.
2. Define and give examples of prompts.
3. Describe the difference between within and extra stimulus prompts.
4. Describe two methods for presenting response prompts.
5. Define and illustrate prompt dependence.
6. Discuss the importance of being aware of instructional demand.
7. Point out the importance of imitation and what you can do to help promote its occurrence.
8. Define physical guidance and graduated guidance, and discuss how and when it should be used.
9. Define and illustrate delayed prompting.
10. Define and illustrated graduated prompting.

11. Define and illustrate fading.
12. Complete this chapter's exercises/activities, or those assigned by your instructor.

*****

One important aspect of providing behavioral services as an RBT will be to teach your clients new behaviors or, in other words, to promote skill acquisition. There are numerous antecedent procedures that can be used to promote skill acquisition. Here, we address some of the more salient ones. Also, Chapter 10 presents several antecedent procedures that can promote skill acquisition while also preventing problem behavior.

Before diving into how to set goals and how to teach skills, we should remember from Chapter 6 that you will need to assess the current level of performance either via an indirect assessment (ask someone), a descriptive assessment (observe in the natural environment and determine to what degree a behavior occurs or not), or a functional analysis (actually present S^Ds and see if the behavior occurs or not). With that refresher, let's look at how to set goals.

Goal Setting

Goal setting *involves specifying your client's performance quality, direction, and/or the required level of performance to be attained. A goal often specifies what is to be accomplished within a specific period of time, or when, where, and with whom it is to occur.* You can set goals during the session with your client as to what order or sequence your client will do the various tasks, how long the break should be, what you might do during the break, and how to earn more break time. Such goals give structure as to what is to occur and when. They function as MOs (motivational operations), and increase the likelihood of your client engaging in the behavior. For example, if your goal is, "I will clean the garage today," the garage is much more likely to get cleaned than without that goal.

Goal setting, though, must be done carefully. Be sure that the goal is not too difficult for your client to accomplish. If you do find that the goal is too difficult, either change goals or create sub-goals (sequential mastery of modified levels of the goal) to teach the desired response in achievable steps. You do not want to pair goal setting with failure. Likewise, do not set goals that are too easy. When they are too easy, the client may find them insulting (or that you must think he or she is stupid), or come to expect only easy tasks. Thus, set challenging but achievable goals.

PROMPTS

As mentioned in Chapter 3, prompts involve substituting an effective but inappropriate S^D for an ineffective but appropriate S^D. For example, in teaching number facts to your client, you could initially provide the answer (i.e., the prompt or inappropriate S^D) with the problem and gradually cover the answer with layers of tracing paper or colored cellophane until your client is able to provide the answer to the problem (i.e., the appropriate S^D) without seeing it. Showing a client how to do something, such as catching a ball, might involve providing a model to be imitated, or an imitative prompt. Telling or reminding your client what or how to do something (e.g., putting his or her clothes away) is providing a prompt. We often rely on providing prompts to help our clients learn a skill and then gradually fade the prompt out to help them function independently of such inappropriate prompts. We want our clients to catch a ball or put away their clothes without constantly being shown or told how to do so. We want the ball and clothes to be the natural S^Ds without having to revert to repeated use of the inappropriate S^D. We want our clients to no longer be dependent on others showing, instructing, or reminding them what they should be doing. They eventually need to become independent of social prompts. Given this is our goal, we must ensure we use prompts appropriately and we must fade them out.

There are two main categories of prompts: stimulus prompts and response prompts: Stimulus prompts are when you either modify the current S^D to make it more salient (within stimulus prompt) or add something to make the S^D more salient (extra stimulus prompt). An example of a within stimulus prompt might be to make the "$1" bigger when trying to get someone to match a picture of a dollar bill among

"$1, $5, and $10." If you were to include an extra stimulus prompt in the same example you might actually put a small picture of a dollar bill with the $1. So with stimulus prompts you modify the stimulus. With response prompts, the RBT provides a behavior prompt (says or does something). For example, response prompts include gesturing, modeling, and physical guidance. In the above example, you might guide the person to match the picture of the dollar bill with the $1.

Presenting Response Prompts

Minimum-to-maximum prompting (or least to most) is one method of presenting prompts that begins with providing the most natural prompt possible. The hierarchy often, but not always, begins with a simple request or physical gestures. If that does not work, you try telling or instructing how to do the skill, then showing how to do the skill, and finally to using physical guidance. The idea is to supply the minimum amount of support necessary and not to move to more intrusive prompts unless necessary. For example, you might request that the client print the letter A. If that does not prompt the behavior, you might try explaining that you make a tepee with a line holding the two sides together. If there is no luck, try showing him how to draw the letter A. Again, if your client still has problems due to how the pencil is held, or with coordination, you can try physical guidance by holding his hand and helping him draw the letter.

Maximum-to-minimum prompting (or most to least), involves starting with a prompt known to evoke the behavior and gradually move on to less intrusive, more naturalistic prompts. This method tends to result in fewer errors and/or failure attempts than the minimum-to-maximum prompting. Thus, if the client can imitate the behavior when shown how to do it, but does not respond well to requests or being told how to do it, modeling is the level at which you would begin your prompting.

Which method to use? One method has not been shown to be more effective than the other. However, this does not mean that both methods will work equally effectively with your client. Clients vary as to which method tends to work the best, so try them both out and discover which tends to work best for your client. But do not haphazardly switch between methods, as this will cause all kinds of confusion for you and your client. However, their effectiveness also may vary with the skill you are trying to teach. So, if one of these methods is not working very well in teaching a particular skill with your client, try the other one.

Be sure to avoid prompt dependence, or **stimulus overdependence**. This prompt or stimulus overdependence is when your client's response becomes dependent on inappropriate or artificial prompts. To help avoid prompt dependence, do not stay at any prompt level too long. Our goal, as mentioned previously, is to fade out prompts and have the natural S^D evoke the behavior to promote independent functioning from social prompts. You should have a fade out plan before using prompts.

Also, consider instructional demand when selecting prompts. **Instructional demand** occurs when the behavior alters based on the way instructions are delivered. For example, your client may be able to do division when the problem is presented as 6/2 = ? but not if presented as 6 ÷ 2 = ? Or another example would be a client we had who did not respond when asked to point to a picture of his dad. Similarly, when asked to point to a picture of his father, he did not respond. However, when the expression used in the home was presented: "Point to your Da Da," he correctly identified the picture of his father. Always try to use prompts or S^Ds that the child is familiar with when assessing for skills, unless you are teaching him to respond to a variety of prompts to help promote generalization.

Two other prompting procedures deserve special attention: Modeling and physical guidance.

Imitative Prompts

There are a number of considerations when using **modeling** (showing the client how to correctly perform the replacement behavior) to prompt the occurrence of the target behavior. First, does you client imitate the behavior of others? If not, teaching your client to imitate should be an important treatment objective. Your client's learning is severely handicapped if he or she does not know how to imitate. You can start by teaching your client to imitate physical movements. This is done by modeling raising your arm and using physical guidance to raise your client's arm above his or her head. Continue doing this while gradually fading out your physical guidance. To avoid or escape from having their arms physically moved, many clients will begin to move their arms to imitate your movement. However, do not depend on negative reinforcement (escaping from having their arm moved) to help teach imitating physical movements. Always apply reinforcement for imitation, or even an approximation to imitating (e.g., partial movement of the arm). Think of how you learned to imitate. Mom and/or dad would say sounds like "ma ma" or "da da." When you first made a similar sound you were reinforced with praise, attention and perhaps affection. After learning to make certain sounds, you learned that they only applied to certain situations: you only got reinforced for calling one person "ma ma," no one else (refer to discrimination training in Chapter 9).

If your client does imitate the behavior of others, check to make sure he knows what behaviors to imitate and not imitate. If he seems to imitate most any behaviors, you will need to teach him to imitate only those behaviors that receive reinforcement, and not those who receive punishment or do not result in reinforcement.

When working with clients who do know how to imitate, there are several things you can do to help foster imitation. These include:

- Provide instructions, rules and a rationale as to why it is important to engage in the behavior.
- Highlight similarities between the model(s) and your client.
- Be sure your client is attending to the modeled behavior.
- Promote practice of the skill through role-play or behavioral rehearsal.
- Ensure simplicity of the behavior to be imitated. In other words, the model may have to demonstrate a component of the behavior and gradually build on it before the complete behavior can be learned. For example, when teaching a golf swing, you might want to model how to hold the club before modeling or teaching the follow-through swing.
- Be sure the model behavior receives reinforcement. You want the client to know that this behavior works. It receives reinforcement.

- Be sure that you and others reinforce the act of imitation. The clients need to know that the behavior works for them too.

Physical Guidance

Physical guidance is another prompting procedure in which another person physically guides a client's appropriate body part(s) through appropriate motions. When you teach infants to feed themselves, you often use physical guidance to guide the spoon into the food and mouth. Physically guidance is often used to teach various swim movements such as the frog kick. It is sometimes used to help teach a golf swing, how to write/print, etc. Once the client begins to get the "feel" of the motion, you gradually fade out the physical guidance. This combination of physical guidance and fading is called graduated guidance. Physical guidance is used after directions, gestures and modeling are found to be insufficient in teaching the skill.

To use physical guidance effectively, you need to obtain the client's cooperation. Resistive clients will not be able to concentrate on the "feel" of the motion. As Mayer et al. (2014) have stated:

> Resist the temptation to use force, because that could incite the individual to become agitated, evoking interfering reactions like struggling to escape, fighting, or crying. Besides being a motivating operation for competing emotional behaviors, using undue pressure is ethically questionable, while excessive force is dangerous! (p. 373).

Thus, if agitated, wait for your client to calm down and guide the movements lightly. Do not use force. If your client continues to resist, talk with your BCBA and possibly work out some sort of relaxation training or pairing the physical guidance with lots of powerful reinforcement.

REDUCING PROMPT DEPENDENCE BY TRANSFERRING STIMULUS CONTROL

We have mentioned several times that our long-range goal is to help our clients become independent of stimulus prompts and social prompts, such a reminders, gestures, physical guidance, modeling, and being instructed or told what to do. Now we look at methods that can help us achieve that goal.

Delayed Prompting

Delayed prompting involves interposing a period of time between the natural S^D (e.g., request) and the prompt, which usually provides the correct response. Usually, the period of time between the S^D and the prompt gradually increases, which is often referred to as progressive delayed prompting. For example, you ask, "What is 3 x 2?" and wait about 3 seconds before giving the answer. Then, you then ask them to repeat the answer and provide praise for doing so. Later, you ask again "What is 3 x 2?" Wait about 5 seconds before giving the answer and have the client repeat the answer again, and you provide praise or some other reinforcer for doing so. You continue this program of gradually increasing the time between the request and providing the prompt or answer until the client provides the answer before the prompt is given. Progressive delayed prompting also is often used with teaching words of a foreign language (ask, "Que es?" and pause), tacting or naming objects, and others. Once your client anticipates or provides the correct response before the prompt is given, that is known as the moment of transfer. The client's response is no longer dependent on the prompt. Stimulus control, or what evokes the behavior, has been transferred to the more natural S^D.

Graduated Prompting (Also known as minimum-to-maximum prompting)

Graduated prompting involves first trying to evoke the behavior with the natural S^D and continuing to progress from least to most intrusive prompts until your wanted response occurs. For example, you might start by asking, "What is 3 x 2?" If there is no response from your client, you might explain, "you need to multiply the 3 times the 2 to get the answer." Again, if there is no response you might try to model solving the problem and then ask the client to imitate what you did. If that does not work, you might then physically guide the client's movements to come up with the correct answer. Another example could be that you ask your client to toss the ball to you. If you do not get a response, you might show them how to toss the ball. Again, if there is no response, you might guide the arm movement that is helping your client toss the ball. Frequently, graduated prompting goes from a verbal request, to giving a direction, to modeling, and then to guided prompting. As your client begins to learn the skill, the client begins to respond before the most intrusive S^D that you are using. As the skill becomes more proficient, your client will eventually respond to the natural S^D before any of the more intrusive prompts are provided. Again, stimulus control, or what evokes the behavior, has been transferred from various prompts to the natural S^D.

Fading

Fading involves gradually moving from maximum prompting to minimal or no prompting. With fading, you start with the prompt that reliably evokes the behavior and gradually fade it out. For example, if you are teaching words that represent colors, and assuming your client knows his colors, you might put the word yellow in yellow, red in red, etc (this is a within stimulus prompt). To teach the word recognition you would gradually fade out the color of each printed word or gradually make each word more and more black until the color is no longer present. If you are using modeling to teach a skill, you would gradually reduce what you are modeling until your client can perform the skill without you showing him or her how to do it. If you are teaching number facts using flash cards, you could put the answer to the number fact on the card and then begin coving the answer. You begin with one layer of tracing paper or colored cellophane, followed by additional layers after several trials at each layer. Again, the idea is to transfer the stimulus control from the answer to the problem presented. As mentioned above, when physical guidance is combined with fading, it is called **graduated guidance**. Here you *gradually reduce the pressure that you are applying to shadowing further and further away until the client can do the skill without any physical guidance*. Usually, when physical guidance is used, it is combined with fading.

No single method of reducing prompt dependence has been shown to be more effective than another. However, that does not mean that one might be more effective for your client than the other methods. You may need to try each of them until you find out the one that works best for client's type of learning. However, an advantage of fading is that when it is used, fewer errors are produced by the client than when the other procedures are use.

Also, recall that stimulus control is developed through differential reinforcement. As an RBT working with a parent or teacher, you will often find that the child has learned a particular behavior with you but continues the inappropriate behavior with the parent or teacher. In such situations, you are the S^{Dr} (see Chapter 3) for the desired behavior, because you have consistently differentially reinforced it. Your client has learned that if he or she engages in the particular desired behavior with you, reinforcement is likely. The parent or teacher also needs to become an S^{Dr} for it. Thus, they must start differentially reinforcing the desired behavior too, so that they will become S^{Dr}s for their child or student to engage in the desired behavior. This topic is further discussed in the next chapter on generalization.

SUMMARY AND CONCLUSIONS

The focus of this chapter was on how to produce independent behavior—behavior that is not dependent on others telling, instructing, showing, or physically guiding your client as to what to do. A behavior cannot be considered learned if your client is still dependent on intrusive prompts, whether you used physical guidance, modeling, maximum to minimum prompting, or minimum to maximum prompting. Thus, several procedures were presented that can be used to help your clients become independent of prompts. These procedures included delayed prompting, graduated prompting, and fading (which also included graduated guidance). Because no single procedure for reducing prompt dependence has been shown to be more effective than another, you will need to discover which works best for each of your clients. Fading does have the advantage of incorporating errorless learning, and most of our clients can do without additional failures. These strategies for transferring stimulus control from intrusive prompts to natural S^Ds help behavior become well established when combined with the generalization and maintenance strategies described in the next chapter.

EXERCISES

After you have completed the exercises below, you will want feedback. Your instructor has access (or can obtain access from the publisher) to sample answers for each of the following exercises:

1. Why is a goal often considered to be an MO?

2. Describe the difference between stimulus and response prompts and develop an example illustrating the various prompts.

3. Which prompting method is best to use when the goal is errorless learning?

4. Describe how instructional demand might influence the effectiveness of your intervention.

5. Discuss why it is important not to use force when using physical guidance.

6. Which is likely to help minimize the occurrence of errors as the client learns a new skill: delayed prompting, graduated prompting or fading?

7. Differentiate between graduated prompting and graduated guidance.

ACTIVITIES

1. Of the procedures described in this chapter for promoting skill acquisition, which have you used before on your behavior or the behavior of others? Describe what you did and be prepared to share.

2. Of the procedures you have not used before, apply each to your behavior, or describe how you would apply each to some other person's behavior.

3. Develop a task analysis (a step-by-step instruction) for how you would implement a Least-to-Most prompting procedure to teach a skill.

4. Develop a task analysis for how you would implement a Most-to-Least prompting procedure to teach a skill.

Chapter 9

Generalization and Maintenance

GOALS

1. Describe the importance of generalization
2. Define and illustrate:
    a. Discrimination training
    b. S^{Dr}
    c. Overgeneralization
    d. Stimulus overselectivity
    e. Stimulus generalization
    f. Response fluency
    g. Continuous reinforcement
    h. Intermittent reinforcement
    i. Behavioral trap
    j. Differentiate between response and stimulus generalization
3. Describe the usefulness of response generalization.

4. Describe and give a rational for at least four methods of producing stimulus generalization.
5. Describe what needs to be considered before asking others to implement the intervention programs in other settings.
6. Describe methods of promoting maintenance.
7. Complete this chapter's exercises/activities, or those assigned by your instructor.

*****

We have talked about how to use behavior analytic procedures to develop skills. However, one thing to remember is the behavior itself must be appropriate to the context or situation in which it occurs. The behavior must be contextually appropriate or suitable for clients and their cultural environment. Although we haven't talked about how to eliminate behavior quite yet, it is important to understand that sometimes it is not about eliminating the behavior completely but making sure it only occurs in appropriate situations. For example, one of our clients, who we will call Joe, would frequently growl. We set up a program that specified that if he wanted to growl, he could do so in his room or bathroom, but not in public (we have set up similar programs for masturbation). Joe began to call his bedroom the "growling room." Eventually, his growling stopped in public. In this example, Joe learned to discriminate in which context the behavior was okay and in which context it was not okay. Think about it—almost any behavior has situations in which it is okay, and situations in which it is not okay to engage. Boxing, or hitting, in the ring is okay but not in the home or classroom. Running is okay outside but not in the house, classroom, church, etc. Thus, behaviors are not inherently good or bad, but their appropriateness varies among situations.

Therefore, children must learn to discriminate in what situations the behavior is appropriate (correct) and in which situations it is not (incorrect). Often, our clients will need to be taught this distinction. Discrimination/generalization training has been recognized as the *most crucial concept and skill* for ABA practitioners-in-training when working with children who have autism (Sulzer-Azaroff, et al., 2008).

Of course, generalization/discrimination training is not only important for children with autism, but it benefits all clients. However, you will find that appropriate discrimination/generalization is often more difficult for children with autism or other intellectual disabilities to learn. As a result, you will often need to place a special focus on this training when working with children who have autism or other intellectual disabilities.

DISCRIMINATION AND GENERALIZATION

Let's start by looking at discrimination, what it is and how to conduct discrimination training.

Discrimination

Discriminative stimuli (S^Ds) are antecedents to a behavior that help your client to know when and where to engage in the behavior. First, remember that specific S^Ds signal to an individual what will happen if they engage in a specific behavior. **S^{Dr}s** are discriminative stimuli that specify to clients the behaviors that are likely to produce reinforcement. They are what encourage or evoke behavior to occur. If S^{Dr}s are not present, your client is not likely to engage in the behavior. When you apply **discrimination training** you are trying to *restrict the variety of S^{Dr}s that evoke the target behavior*. The client, Joe, learned to discriminate to growl only in his room, while others learn to masturbate only in private, and so on. Thus, when teaching discrimination, we assure that the behavior is only reinforced in the presence of certain stimuli and not reinforced in the presence of any other stimuli. You can use discrimination training when you want to teach a child that a red object is identified with the word, "red." While holding the red object, ask the child, "What color?" Ensure that you only reinforce the correct response, "red." Therefore, if the child responded, "red," to a blue item, we would not deliver reinforcement. Similarly, if we held the red item and asked the child, "what color," we would not deliver reinforcement for the answer, "blue." By *only* delivering reinforcement when the child identifies the color red correctly and denying reinforcement for all incorrect answers, we are teaching the child to discriminate the color red.

Sometimes, when training clients, we are faced with a situation where the client is not discriminating when we want them to. For example, if a child calls all men, "da da" (a behavior referred to as **overgeneralization**), we must make sure that he is only reinforced for the response, "da da," when said in the presence of his father, and he is not reinforced when said in the presence of other men. By doing so, the child soon learns to discriminate saying, "da da," only in the presence of his father. By using differential reinforcement we restricted the variety of S^D's that evoked the response, "da da," to one, his father.

The opposite of discrimination is generalization. In the newspaper, we noticed a cartoon that illustrates this occurrence of generalization. The infant said, "da da," when the father was present, so Dad commented on how she must get her smarts from her father. The wife then commented that their child also called the toilet, "da da." The father responded, "buzz-killer."

Generalization

Response generalization. With respect to generalization, we break it up into two different types: Response generalization and stimulus generalization. In brief, **response generalization** *refers to a client engaging in a different response under the same stimulus condition.* For example, writing may vary somewhat when the child writes the word red when the RBT holds up a red item and asks, "what color?" Or, a young child is asked to draw a straight line—some lines will be straighter than others. Response generalization makes the use of shaping more possible. For example, when teaching a child to draw a straight line, as the child learns one approximation toward a straight line. Eventually, other approximations, or straighter lines, appear that allow us to select closer approximations to our straight line. Or, in response to the question, "How are you?" the child responds, "good," "fine," or "okay." Again, the child is engaging in different responses under the same stimulus condition.

Stimulus generalization. In **stimulus generalization**, *the response remains the same, but the stimulus or stimuli changes.* In other words, the behavior occurs in the presence of different stimuli such as different settings, people, and time of day. For example, the child says, "red," during training with the RBT and whenever the parent holds up or points to a red item and asks, "What color?" The thing to remember is the term that comes before the word "generalization" (either "response" or "stimulus") tells you what is going to be different (response = different responses, same stimulus; stimulus = different stimuli, same response). You will be using stimulus generalization more than response generalization, so that is the topic we address below.

Teaching stimulus generalization. It is important to note that just because you want generalization does *not* mean it will happen without being taught. Just like with discrimination, some learners struggle with generalization. For example, a client with autism, whom we will call Refugio, was taught in a therapy room to touch his nose, head, mouth, etc. upon request. The male BCBA, Jim, reported this improvement to the female teacher, Sue. However, when Sue requested him to touch his head, etc., the child did not do so. She reported this to Jim, who told her maybe he had to be present. Sue then made the various requests in his presence without success. Then, Jim tried making the requests of Refugio. Again, Refugio did not display compliance. The requests were not functioning as S^{Dr}s like they did in Jim's therapy room. Jim continued to try different stimuli, or environmental changes. Jim finally found out that if the table and chair were present from the therapy room, the child would touch the appropriate body part upon request. This phenomenon in which *the behavior is controlled by one or more non-relevant stimuli* is called **stimulus overselectivity**. This is one of the reasons that generalization is such an important skill that should be addressed at the start of teaching and/or services. Generalization training reduces the likelihood of stimulus overselectivity occurring. Let's look at how we can promote stimulus generalization.

Stimulus Generalization *involves developing a variety of relevant S^{Dr}s that will evoke the behavior*. Most of the behaviors you will teach you will want to occur in the presence of a variety of *people, situations*, and *times*. Thus, rather than restricting the variety of S^{Dr}s, as with discrimination training, generalization training *expands the variety of S^{Dr}s that evoke a behavior*. So, what are some things you can do to help promote generalization across people, situations and times?

First, it is important that you *plan for generalization from the beginning* by including as part of your clients' objectives the situations, times, and in the presence of which people you want the behaviors you are teaching to occur. For example, Frankie is to look at the face of the person who is talking with her at least 30 percent of the time during the conversation for two consecutive occurrences during each of *various times of the day, involving parents, RBT, friends, home visitors, and when she is at school.*

Next, you need to incorporate generalization training. There are a number of strategies you can use to help promote generalization:

Have other people reinforce the target behavior. Generally speaking, the person who provides the reinforcement to the client's behavior becomes an S^{Dr} to engage in that behavior. If you are the only one who reinforces the target behavior (e.g., sharing, demonstrating good sportsmanship by complimenting others for improvement, good plays, winning), the target behavior might only occur in your presence. Your clients have learned that they are likely to get reinforced for doing those behaviors when you are present. You are the S^{Dr}. However, we want others to serve as S^{Dr}s in the environment, so the target behavior will occur in their presence too. Thus, you need to get them to prompt and reinforce the occurrence of the target behavior (e.g., sharing, etc.), so they, too, will more likely function as S^{Dr}s. By doing so, you are increasing the variety of S^{Dr}s that will evoke the behavior and encouraging stimulus generalization. If those in the home and school do not reinforce the newly occurring behavior, it will not persist in your absence.

A caution. Be careful in what you ask the parents and others to do. Some are more skillful than others in delivering reinforcement. Those who tend to not provide much reinforcement will have a more difficult time following your request. You should model and role-play the skill with them before you have them do it on their own. Also, we have found it helpful to specify exact situations in which they are to provide the reinforcement (when he first gets up, during breakfast, etc.), and gradually increase the variety of those situations as they become more comfortable in delivering reinforcement. Be sure to provide recognition for their improved use of reinforcement. When possible, get the spouse and others to provide recognition for program implementation, and point out how it is influencing their child's behavior. Research has shown that the child's behavior change by itself is often not a sufficient reinforcer for the parent or teacher to use the procedure. Parents and teachers also need to receive reinforcement from others for doing so. Thus, *as a behavior technician, get in the habit of delivering reinforcement to caregivers in addition to your client.*

Another way to promote generalization is to *teach the behavior sequentially, first in one environment, then the next, then the next, etc.* For example, this strategy has been used with 4- to 6-year-old boys with autism to initiate conversations with peers in the presence of toys. However, conversations did not occur when novel toys were introduced. There was not an increase in conversation until the boys were provided training with a variety of different toys. This illustration reminds us that not only do we have to be aware of the social cues in the environment, but also the physical cues (situations). When you are successful in teaching the skill in one situation after another, you are associating more antecedent stimuli with the behavior and its reinforcers. Many of these antecedents are likely to begin to develop into S^{Dr}s for your client, thereby increasing the S^{Dr}s that evoke the behavior and promoting stimulus generalization. This also makes it more likely that some of these S^{Dr}s may be present in other environments, making generalization more likely to occur in them. Thus, *provide practice in the skill to be generalized in a variety of settings (e.g., school, home, community settings).*

Strive for common S^{Dr}s. *Generalization is more likely to occur under similar antecedent stimuli rather than in similar environments.* This will likely happen when there are common S^{Dr}s present in the similar environments. Strive for similarities of materials, schedules of reinforcement, types of reinforcers used, etc. Set up the training environment to mimic the natural environment as closely as you can. The greater the similarities between the environment in which you teach the behavior and those to which you want it to generalize, the greater the likelihood that there will be common S^{Dr}s to evoke its occurrence. For example, one of the authors is training a client how to order, receive their food, and pay at a local sandwich shop. The first step in training was to make a corner of the classroom look like the local shop and include things seen in the shop. We included a cash register, a menu, and even went as far as having the RBT wear a hat from the shop when running the program. In other words, we used stimuli from the generalization setting (the actual sandwich shop) within our training setting (classroom) to help promote generalization.

Another way to promote generalization is to *achieve response fluency.* **Response fluency** exists when t*he client's behavior occurs smoothly, rapidly, with little apparent effort.* Your client is less likely to try the target behavior in novel environments when it takes effort to engage in the behavior, and/or your client does not yet feel comfortable engaging in it. However, if the behavior is very proficient and can be done easily, it is more likely to occur in other environments. This is the premise behind learning your times tables — the more fluent you are the more likely you will be able to use this skill in other environments (e.g., calculating the size of a room before determining the amount of tiles you will need to replace your floor). If your client is struggling to master fluency of a goal, offer many opportunities to practice this new skill while receiving reinforcement until it becomes easy and effortless.

Teach techniques to mediate generalization. There are several techniques that you can use to help many of your clients learn to generalize once response fluency has been achieved. One technique is to teach them to come up with goals as to where, when and with whom they will engage in the behavior. For example, they might develop goals such as: "When I eat some popcorn, I will share with my sister," or "When I play the board game with my sister, I will take turns." Guide your client to create goals that are practical skills, used in many natural setting throughout a typical day, appropriate for the client's age level, and promote social engagement with all types of peers. These goals often serve as MOs to help motivate the client to generalize the behavior.

For your clients who are able to count their own behavior, you can have them record occurrences of it in various setting. If you select this strategy, be sure to reinforce your clients at times for accurate recording of their own behavior. Self-recording appears to help clients focus on their own behavior, thereby achieving more awareness and control over it. If your client is able to comprehend the interventions in place for him or her, it is beneficial to explain what the tactics being used are and their functional significance. Setting goals creates a way to jointly establish those interventions in a way your client understands and agrees with.

Also, involve your clients in selecting where, when and with whom they will try the behavior next. This activity helps them begin to learn generalization as a general skill that, with hope, they begin to practice more and more on their own. Be sure to encourage and reinforce such practice.

Once they have practiced the skill in the new environment, teach them to self-reinforce their attempts (e. g. "I did it," or, "I did well"). Parents, teachers and other contingency managers do not always remember to reinforce the new behavior that is being generalized. Self-reinforcement can help bridge this extinction (or lack of reinforcement) gap.

Finally, it is also a good idea to *teach your clients how to solicit reinforcers in new environments*. Not only do you need to ask those in other environments to be sure to look for the behavior's occurrences, but it is helpful if the client knows acceptable ways of prompting for reinforcement. You can teach your verbal clients to make statements such as, "How am I doing?" "I'm done," or, "How's this?" You can teach these skills to your clients by using modeling, role-playing, feedback, and, of course, reinforcement.

MAINTENANCE

As you recall, when teaching a behavior, you want to try to *reinforce it each time it occurs*. This schedule of reinforcement is called **Continuous Reinforcement**, or **CRF**. However, once the behavior has been taught and is getting close to fluency, gradually begin to decrease the frequency of reinforcer delivery. *When some, not all, of the correct occurrences are reinforced*, this is called **Intermittent Reinforcement**. One reason for switching from a CRF to an intermittent schedule is that there is rarely a behavior that occurs in the real world that gets reinforced every time it occurs. Moreover, by switching from a CRF to an intermittent schedule, you are making the behavior more resistant to extinction (when it does not produce reinforcement). Thus, we use various schedules of intermittent reinforcement to gradually thin out the frequency of reinforcer delivery. Again, the purpose of gradually thinning out the reinforcers is to increase the likelihood that the behavior will maintain its occurrence in the natural environment. Remember reinforcement in the natural environment tends to not be consistent or frequent (think of your own behavior and how often it is reinforced). In fact, extinction conditions often exist. For the client to maintain the newly established behavior, the behavior must survive those various periods of no reinforcement. It is your job to help teach your clients to weather the non-reinforcement periods. As mentioned, you do this by gradually thinning out the frequency of reinforcement that is provided. Here are some suggestions to help you move toward maintenance of the target behavior.

When teaching for maintenance may not be necessary. Sometimes you do not need to do much of anything and teaching through scheduled reinforcement is unnecessary. This tends to occur when:

- The new replacement behavior is easier than the old behavior.
- The new behavior produces faster results.
- The new behavior is valued by the natural environment and produces praise and recognition from significant others.
- The client is proficient in self-reinforcement.

When this occurs it is often called a **behavioral trap**. *The natural contingencies took over control, or trapped the behavior.*

Teaching for maintenance. Most often, though, we do need to teach maintenance. There are a variety of things you can do to help promote maintenance:

> *Do not withdraw or thin the reinforcers too abruptly.* If you withdraw them too abruptly, it will be like introducing extinction (e. g. receiving no reinforcement), and the behavior is likely to disappear. Similarly, introduce delay of the reinforcer delivery (e. g. increase the amount of time between the correct response and the delivery of reinforcement) gradually. We all must learn delay of gratification.

Try to assure that competing behaviors do not get reinforced. A behavior is not likely maintained if competing behaviors are getting reinforced. For example, you have taught a child to request an item rather than point and whine for it, but the family still gives the child the item when he points and whines. Your client is not likely to maintain the requesting behavior with those family members, because he has learned that pointing and whining will serve the same function. Similarly, reinforcing competing behaviors can prevent maintenance when teaching a child to raise her hand to request or make a comment. If the teacher often takes the comments of those students who blurt out, hand-raising is not likely to maintain. Plus, in both situations, the S^{Dr}s for the undesired behaviors are still alive and well.

Try to make sure that the newly acquired behaviors do not receive punishment. If you start a client on a new exercise program and overdo it, their bodies will feel the punishment in the form of very sore muscles. Similarly, be sure siblings or peers do not punish the new behavior. "Look, Mike is kissing up to the teacher again." Also, when helping a parent implement an extinction program, there is likely to be a transitory increase in the child's problem behavior before it decreases (e. g. an extinction burst). This is punishment for the parent's use of extinction. You not only need to prepare the parent for this happening but provide extra support, reinforce continued program implementation, and make sure that the child's acceptable alternative behaviors are being reinforced.

Achieve fluency before thinning the reinforcers too much. As mentioned previously, if the behavior no longer requires much effort, and occurs rapidly and accurately, the child is much more willing to try it out and maintain it in other settings. The child is less likely to engage in the behavior if it feels awkward, or the client is not at ease doing it.

Teach self-management skills. Again, teach self-recording and self-reinforcement. They can help with maintenance the same way they do with generalization. Self-recording helps them become more aware of when they are expected to engage in the behavior and when they are not, while self-reinforcement helps to minimize the effects of extinction conditions or withholding reinforcement.

Use indiscriminate contingencies. As you thin your reinforcer delivery, generally it is best to not stick to a fixed schedule. Consequently, the client cannot predict after which response reinforcement will be delivered when it is delivered intermittently (e.g., after every second response, or after every two minutes). Instead, vary the reinforcer delivery schedule (e.g., after one response, after three, after two, etc.), so the client can't predict when the next reinforcer may occur.

SUMMARY AND CONCLUSIONS

An objective is not truly achieved until the target behavior has been generalized to all relevant people, places, and times of day. You also need to show that it is being maintained in those situations without frequent reinforcement. Once you master the material in this chapter, you will know how to help teach a behavior to occur and persist in various appropriate environments. *It is not enough to just teach a behavior, but the real test is ensuring its persistence in the situations in which it needs to occur.*

EXERCISES

After you have completed the exercises below, you will want feedback. Your instructor has access (or can obtain access from the publisher) to sample answers for each of the following exercises:

1. Develop or modify an objective to include the situations, times, and people for which you want the behavior to occur.
2. List at least three explanations for failure of a trained behavior to generalize.

3. Identify some possible S^{D}'s that are common across: 1. backyard and school playground; 2. special education classroom and regular classroom,
4. Compare and contrast stimulus generalization and maintenance.
5. Identify what is likely to lead to relapse or no maintenance.
6. Can new behaviors maintain without programming for maintenance? If so, explain how.

ACTIVITIES

1. Design a relapse prevention program for a behavior of your own that you have recently changed. Describe what you did and how well it worked. Compare your relapse prevention programs with others.
2. Select a behavior that you have recently learned and teach yourself to mediate generalization. Describe the programs that you used to achieve generalization for your behavior. (To become skillful in generalizing, practice generalizing several of your behaviors—e.g., I learned X in class, now I'm going to practice it in x and y settings. If possible, compare your results with that of others.

Chapter 10

Preventing Problem Behavior Through Introducing and Modifying Antecedents

GOALS

1. Define and illustrate:
    a. MOs
    b. S^{Dr}s
    c. Behavioral momentum
    d. Response demand
    e. Functional skill level
    f. Interspersal technique
    g. Fluency
    h. Providing choice
    i. Redirection
    j. Distracting with preferred events or items

k. Participative goal setting
   l. Activity Schedule
   m. Modeling, including how to use it effectively
   n. Social Stories
   o. NCR
3. Describe several methods of reducing the complexity or difficulty of a task and point out why this may be important to do.
4. Describe why developing reinforcing environments are important.
5. Describe how each of the interventions described in this chapter can serve as MOs.
6. Complete this chapter's exercises/activities, or those assigned by your instructor

*****

One of the best interventions for addressing inappropriate behavior is to modify or change the events that happen before (i.e., antecedents) the inappropriate behavior to help *prevent* its occurrence. Let's take the example of a child who tantrums (e.g., screams, bites, hits, kicks, and elopes) when he is requested to transition to, or asked to do a low preference activity (homework, learning colors, sitting on the toilet, etc.). There are a number of research-based possible antecedent interventions that you can use to help prevent the likelihood of such behavior occurring. They each have the potential to serve as motivational operations (MOs) that help the requested task become more reinforcing and/or less punitive. Remember also, that sometimes individuals engage in behavior to get access to someone or something. Antecedent interventions can be used to decrease someone's motivation for a particular person or thing. For example, a student is the class clown to get his friends' attention in the classroom. If, at the beginning of the day you provide a short "hang out with your friends" time, chances are the student will not be motivated to act out in class. Getting lots of attention from his friends before going into the room will decrease the student's need for attention during class. Likewise, students will be less likely to engage in the inappropriate behavior if they "hang out" because you give them a more appropriate way to get the same feeling that peer attention provides.

Motivational Operations

One way to prevent someone from engaging in problem behavior is to change the value of what they are getting or get out of doing the behavior. This kind of modification is called an **MO intervention**. **MOs** are *antecedent events that change the value of the consequence along with the immediate discriminative stimulus (S^D)*. For example making homework less aversive for your client by either reducing the amount or difficulty of the homework, or letting her have a snack while she does her homework, can reduce her motivation to get out of the task. Similarly, if a child hopes to gain your attention by knocking things off the shelf in the grocery store, giving him undivided attention before going into the store can reduce his "need" for attention in the store. These solutions work because they change the value of the consequence of the problem behavior: getting out of homework is less reinforcing and getting attention is not so necessary in the store.

Discriminative Stimuli (S^Ds)

Another event that occurs before a behavior is a stimulus that "tells" or signals what will happen if a behavior occurs. There are several types of discriminative stimuli. The type discussed in this chapter is referred to as an S^{Dr}. An S^{Dr} is an antecedent that tends to evoke a particular response because reinforcement has followed the response in the past in the presence of the antecedent stimulus (that became the S^{Dr}). For example, Refugio goofs off, Johnny laughs. This laughter serves as a reinforcer for Refugio's goofing off. What is the S^{Dr} for goofing off? It's Johnny. So, if we placed Johnny across the room or removed him from the situation, the S^{Dr} is no longer present to signal that goofing off will get reinforced. MOs and S^{Dr}s are further illustrated below in the following interventions. Sometimes removing the item that is used to produce the stimulation can be effective in reducing automatically-maintained behavior. In other words, removing the S^{Dr} will remove the signal that if the individual engages in the response it will be reinforcing. For example, a child with autism waves a string in front of his face because he finds the visual stimulation it produces reinforcing. If the string is not around, the signal for waving it is not around.

USING MOTIVATING OPERATIONS TO HELP PREVENT PROBLEM BEHAVIOR

Use Behavioral Momentum

This procedure is utilized when the individual engages in problem behavior to escape or avoid engaging in an aversive event. *Try using requests to engage in several high preference activities just before requesting your client to engage the low preference activity.* The sequential presentation of tasks that they are likely to comply with before a non-preferred activity creates a momentum of compliance. Thus, using this intervention is more likely to result in clients complying with the request to engage in the low preference activity. Also, be sure to reinforce each instance of compliance. For example, "Jimmy, please feed the fish. Great job! Thanks for feeding them." Next, "Please draw me a picture. "Fantastic job. I like the colors you chose. Very pretty." "Let's play a little catch. Nice throw. Great catch. You sure know how to play catch well." "OK, let's do a little bit of simple math" (the low preference activity) "and then we can do your favorite activity." (When you are making so many requests, it is essential to use differential reinforcement. You must reinforce correct behavior, while denying reinforcement to any incorrect behavior.) Another example of using behavioral momentum when teaching a new skill, or a cognitive skill such as math, is to start with easier items, items you know your client can do, to help build the behavioral momentum. This initial string of reinforced successes appears to encourage the client to persist with the more difficult ones. Identify the MO and the S^{Dr} that were used in this math example.

Reduce Response Demand

Again, this antecedent intervention is for behavior that is caused by escaping or avoiding demands. *Reducing the amount of time and effort required to engage in the activity* can reduce the likelihood of problematic reactions. However, if it is important to teach the client to remain on a task for a set period of time, gradually increase the time involved in the activity after the response demand has been implemented. For example, if the activity is a pencil and paper task, cover up much of the assignment and say, "Let's just do this much, and then we can do X (a high preference activity). If it is a 20-minute activity, cut it down to 5 or 10 minutes (i.e., "If you can do this for 5 minutes, then we can do X"). As the client demonstrates that he does his work satisfactorily during the 5 minutes over two consecutive sessions, gradually start to increase the amount of the task he is required to do (e.g., from 25% to 50% to 80% to 100%). The amount of the increase is determined by the client's performance. For some clients, the increase will need to be more gradual to help ensure success. For others, the increase can be larger (e.g., from 25% to 70% to 100%). Again, note that the punitive nature of the task was reduced initially by reducing the time and effort required to do the task. As a result, using this intervention strategy can often reduce problematic reactions to your requests.

Reduce Complexity or Difficulty of Task

A major factor that evokes elopement and tantrums maintained by escape/avoidance is asking individuals to engage in a task or activity above (or below) their functional level. The **functional skill level** is *the performance level at which the individual is able to attain consistent success*. Frequently, such problem behavior can be avoided by *adjusting the task to match the client's functional skill level*. This can involve teaching prerequisite skills (e.g., teaching addition and subtraction prior to multiplication, holding the pencil correctly before printing one's name, paying attention before teaching imitation) or reducing the size or complexity of the task (as described in the response demand section above). Another intervention which temporarily reduces the complexity of the task involves *interspersing easier tasks or items among those that are more challenging*—this is called the **interspersal technique**. For example, when a child who has learned to add 1 to the numbers 1 through 10, and must now add 2 to the numbers 1 through 10, try interspersing problems of adding 1 to the numbers 1 through

10 among those of adding 2. This strategy makes the task easier, provides extra practice to develop **fluency** (*the behavior occurs rapidly, smoothly, and with little effort*), retention, and helps to make the activity less aversive and more reinforcing. (A skill is not really learned until it occurs fluently.) Also, start the task with items that you know your client can do to *build behavioral momentum*. As a result of using these interventions, individuals tend to accomplish more and remain on task longer.

Provide Choice

When choice is provided it functions as an MO that improves the effectiveness of the reinforcers being used, and may, in itself, be reinforcing. It helps to prevent problem behaviors, particularly for individuals whose problem behaviors are escape or access motivated. Provide choice, then, among high preference reinforcers that your clients can work for ("Which do you want to work for—playing the game on your iPad or playing with your Legos?"). Also provide choice when determining the sequence in which your clients are required to complete their tasks. (e.g., "Which do you want to do next, your math or break?") With access motivated behavior, if an item is not available, give the individual a choice between other reinforcing items. For example, if a child wants access to his musical toy, but it is not available because you are in the library, ask the child if he wants an available activity (e.g., reading a book or coloring). It is very important that if the child picks one of the choices without engaging in problem behavior, praise her for not engaging in the problem behavior.

Provide Redirection

Sometimes a client is not attending to a task or is engaged in some inappropriate behavior. A common technique to use is to redirect her back to the task or a more acceptable alternative behavior. For example, some children engage in a chain of responses (see Chapter 8 on Chaining) before they start hitting, throwing things, or engaging in other aggressive behavior. Such a chain might start off with a deep sigh, followed by stopping their work or breaking a pencil. Next, they might toss some work on the floor, begin to swear, and then become aggressive. Try to re-direct early in the chain of events to prevent the occurrence of the aggression. Also, rather than telling a youngster to stop doing something, redirect him to another activity. Noncompliance is more likely when you request that the child stop an activity than when you request him to start one. You can effectively eliminate problem behavior that is automatically reinforcing, if you block the behavior and redirect the client to another behavior (this procedure is called *response interruption* and *response redirection*). Be careful, though, when using redirection. It does not work in all situations. For example, it usually is best not to use it when the child is misbehaving for attention, in that redirection does provide attention. In other words, if you use redirection, when the client is acting out for attention, your redirection is likely to reinforce, or increase, the occurrence of the acting out behavior in the future.

Distract with Preferred Events or Items

Individuals with autism, as well as many others, are likely to engage in problem behavior when asked to transition to a less-preferred activity, or to less structured surroundings. Providing the client freedom to choose the next activity can help, but it is also helpful to distract the child with a preferred item. For example, you can distract them by letting them hold a favorite toy or engaging in a high preference activity during transitioning (e.g., watching a video, talking to a favorite peer, playing iPad games, etc.). In other words, distract the client with a preferred item or activity during transitions to a less-preferred activity. The same idea can work if a child's inappropriate behavior is maintained by attention. If you know you are going to be on an important phone call and will not be able to give a child attention, you can set her up with a preferred activity or item to distract her from wanting attention while you are on the phone. It is important that the distractor yields more reinforcement than the problem behavior. Also, ensure that you are not presenting the distractor when the client is engaging in the problem to avoid reinforcing unwanted behaviors.

Use Participative Goal Setting

This antecedent intervention is similar to providing choice, because it involves your client as a participant in choosing what goals to address in advance. However, not all clients are at a cognitive level to participate in goal setting. For those who are able to participate in goal-setting, it can be empowering for them to have a sense of control over programs. For example, in developing response fluency (see Chapters 7 & 8), try involving your clients in setting goals as to how fast they can do the activity (e.g., math facts, color recognition, etc). Also, ask your clients what areas they need to improve and jointly select goals, rather than dictating all the goals. Such joint goal setting has been shown to improve both compliance and performance.

Use An Activity Schedule

An **activity schedule** *specifies in words, or displays in pictures, the daily sequence of activities your client is to complete for the session.* Each listing on the activity schedule serves as an S^{Dr} to prompt what your client will do next. Activity schedules provide greater structure, help your clients prepare for what will happen next, and help make the expectations clear. They also provide an opportunity to introduce choice (e.g., "Which of these shall we do next?"). As a result, activity schedules have been shown to reduce transition-related acting out behaviors and noncompliance. With that said, activity schedules only work if you differentially reinforce the client for following the activity schedule (see Chapter 11 for how to use differential reinforcement).

Consider Using a Timer and First/Then Statements

Two other strategies that have often been shown to work effectively in helping clients to remain on task are:

1. Set a timer as to when the activity will start, and reinforce the client for coming as soon as it rings. Soon the timer becomes and S^{Dr} to prompt him to do the next activity.

2. Use the phrase, "First we finish this, then we can do ____." This sets it up so that the client knows as soon as the task is finished, not before, he will be able to do the more preferred activity.

Use Modeling

Modeling was addressed in Chapter 8 to teach skills. When you, or preferably cooperative peers or siblings demonstrate *how to behave*, be sure to provide reinforcement to their modeled behaviors. Also, when your clients imitate the behavior, reinforce their acts of imitation. Let's suppose you are trying to help teach some clients to play catch, but they tend to throw the ball too hard. Have friends or siblings play catch with you and provide reinforcement for appropriate throwing. Then ask your clients to play again and to throw the ball like their friends or siblings did. When you see your clients engaging in a minor infraction (e.g., yelling too loudly, not using the equipment properly, or not following the rules of the game, use the minor infraction as a prompt for you to look for others who are engaged in the appropriate behavior and reinforce that behavior. Be sure to reinforce when your clients imitate that behavior, because that is the behavior you want to teach or replace the infraction.

Modeling or showing how to do a skill is a very commonly used procedure. We have also used it as part of a video modeling training procedure to teach when and how to cross the street safely, how to tie a shoe, how to put on a shirt, when and how to greet another, etc. (see Chapters 7 & 8). You can even use your clients at times as their own model by videotaping their exemplary performance (if necessary, edit out any mistakes or poor performance) to show them what they can do. Let's look at an example with attention maintained behavior in the classroom and how you could use modeling. Hillary blurts out answers in class to get the teacher's attention. One thing you could do is show Hillary a video of a student raising her hand and getting called on before answering the question. In addition, when other kids raise their hands in class, the teacher could give them attention.

Modeling is a very effective procedure in teaching how to behave, but it is more likely to work effectively when you follow the guidelines we presented in Chapter 8 for using modeling.

Use Appropriate Social Stories

Social stories usually address a specific social behavior, are written in the first person, and are designed to teach the child the who, what, where, when, and why of the social behavior. They often include pictures or video of the social interaction tailored to the child's situation and ability. Many social stories can be found on the Internet. Social stories might be used to help teach a child to "stay on the topic" of a current discussion. Also, it can teach the client how to say "Hi" or use the bathroom appropriately. To ensure maximal effectiveness, be sure the desired behavior is reinforced in the story, reinforce its occurrence whenever the client engages in it, prompt the behavior's occurrence, and provide opportunities to practice the skill (e.g., use role playing). In other words, use a social story as a model of how to behave and not behave, and follow the guidelines from Chapter 8 for using effective modeling. It is important to note that just reading the stories will not change behavior—you must role-play, practice the new skill, and provide differential reinforcement contingent on its occurrence.

Provide a Highly Reinforcing Environment

People tend to seek out reinforcing environments and avoid or escape from punitive ones. We know that reinforcing environments help to reduce problem behavior (e.g., disruptions, tantrums) and increase pro-social behavior (e.g., on-task, production). Studies have shown us that increased rates of positive reinforcement result in less problem behavior, such as tantrums, aggression, vandalism, and more spontaneous initiations. Simply adding toys to a sterile environment resulted in less self-injury maintained by sensory stimulation. Even something as effortless as greeting children and providing each child with a compliment has been shown to get the children not to seek out attention in inappropriate ways, start a task sooner, and spend more time on the task.

A procedure often used to help promote a more reinforcing environment is **Non-Contingent Reinforcement**, or **NCR**. NCR is *providing reinforcers periodically, on a frequent basis (e.g., an average of every five minutes) regardless of what the child is doing.* However, if the client is engaged in a problem behavior in most applied settings (e.g., home and school), the reinforcer is withheld for a brief amount of time so that it does not immediately follow the problem behavior (e.g., wait 10 seconds). NCR has been shown to reduce a wide variety of problem behaviors. For example, if the clients frequently receive non-contingent attention they are less likely to act out for attention. Aversive environments and/or activities become less aversive, resulting in less escape-related problem behavior. If access to a variety of activities is available, there is no need to act out to obtain them. Generally, an increase in the levels of reinforcement and a more supportive environment of desired behavior can result in the decrease of problem behavior. So, in addition to contingent reinforcement, use NCR combined with extinction and other preventive interventions to avoid inadvertently reinforcing problem behaviors as an effective way to reduce or eliminate challenging behavior.

Let's look at an example so you get an idea of how to implement NCR. Kay is a stay-at-home mom with two children under the age of five, Lynn and Ben. Ben has a communication delay and does not speak. When Ben's mom is busy cooking dinner and he wants her attention, what does he do? He knows that if he hits his sister mom will stop what she is doing and give him attention (e.g., she tells him to stop hitting his sister and to play nice). After meeting with a BCBA, Ben's mother decides to give NCR a try. So, before starting dinner the next day she sits down with Lynn and Ben and plays with them, gives them attention, and tells them how much she loves it when they play nice. Then, when she goes to cook dinner she sets her egg timer for five minutes. When it dings, she goes back to where the children are playing, gives them each a kiss on the head, and tells them how she loves it when they play together. She goes back into the kitchen and sets the timer again for another five minutes. Again, when it dings she walks into the playroom and gives both children attention and tells them how proud she is that they are getting along. She keeps doing this until dinner is ready. By providing non-contingent attention every five minutes, she reduced the need for Ben to act out for attention. At dinner she tells they can have their favorite dessert, because they played together so nicely while she made dinner (this last part is contingent reinforcement).

A final suggestion to help improve your rapport with your client.: Always positively greet your client when you arrive, and start your session with something fun. Also end the session with something fun or reinforcing. By providing this NCR, the client is more likely to find the relationship reinforcing and be excited when you come to the home, school, or residential setting.

SUMMARY AND CONCLUSIONS

You might ask how, or why, do more reinforcing environments help prevent so many problem behaviors? If your clients are receiving more reinforcement, they are less likely to engage in escape-related behaviors (e.g., elopement, aggression). The task is not as punitive because it is paired with reinforcement. They are less likely to act out to obtain reinforcers because they are already receiving them. Thus, use the above-mentioned interventions and draw heavily from the chapters on reinforcement and differential reinforcement to provide that highly reinforcing environment.

All the antecedent interventions mentioned above tend to make it more likely that your client will comply with your request. Thus, each can be used to modify the MO to help your request to function as a discriminative stimulus (S^{Dr}). Each is also likely to decrease the punitive nature of the requested task and/or increase the value of your selected reinforcers. Use them freely, but also be sure to follow your client's compliance with effective differential reinforcement. Once the target behavior is well established, gradually reduce the antecedent interventions, other prompts, and the reinforcers that you are providing. Remember these antecedent interventions work well for behavior maintained by all sources of reinforcement (social positive = to get something, social negative = to get out of something, and automatic = because it feels good). You may also need to request your BCaBA or BCBA to provide you with extra training (e.g., modeling) on any of the interventions you are not skilled in implementing.

EXERCISES

After you have completed the exercises below, you will want feedback. Your instructor has access (or can obtain access from the publisher) to sample answers for each of the following exercises:

1. You are helping several clients to remain on task when doing their homework. Describe how you would use behavioral momentum, reducing response demand, choice, and the interspersal technique.
2. Your client tends to resist transitioning to lower preference activities. Which of the strategies in this chapter might be good to use? Also describe how each might be applied.
3. When watching television, Jake bites his cuticles until they bleed. A BACB has conducted a functional analysis and determined that he does it because of automatic reinforcement. The BCBA wants you to implement a NCR program, where he has access to something to bite noncontingently while he watches television. How would you go about implementing this NCR procedure?
4. Pauline engages in problem behavior in school to get peer attention. The BCBA wants you to implement NCR attention in the classroom to reduce her motivation for peer attention. You know that your attention or the teacher's attention is not very reinforcing. How could you get her peers to implement NCR?

ACTIVITIES

The parent and/or the behavior technician (BT) can implement the following two activities. However, they will have their greatest impact if the parents or caregivers implement them. Thus, they are written to the caregiver, so that you can use them to assist the caregiver in developing a more reinforcing home environment. However, for this activity, do them on your own behavior and/or that of a friend's. (i.e., Where it says "child," insert your name or that of your friend's name.)

1. Look for and Positively Recognize Positive or Desired Behavior. This technique, called positive scanning, often helps to promote a reinforcing environment. For example, if

you observe your children sharing or trading a toy cooperatively, praise them both. If your child climbs in the car and immediately hooks his own seat belt, compliment him for being safe. So often we find ourselves responding primarily to inappropriate or irritating behavior with disapproving comments. Positive scanning will help to increase the positive comments while decreasing the negative ones. Set up prompts (e.g., reminders such as posted notes) to use this technique not only with your children, but with your significant others, also. See if the interpersonal relationships tend to improve. They often do, if you faithfully implement this technique.

2. Create a Positive Behavior Chart. List five to ten behaviors your child does spontaneously that you can positively recognize. Leave room to place checkmarks, stars, or various stickers next to each of them. Place the list, or S^{Dr}, on the refrigerator or on a bulletin board. Place a check mark, star or sticker next to each behavior each time you positively recognize it. Keep track for a several days or a week and see if those behaviors start happening more often. Below is a sample Positive Behavior Chart. List the behaviors in place of the sample ones that apply to your or your friend.

Positive Behavior	Stars, checks, stickers, etc	Comments
Got dressed by herself		
Shared a toy with her brother		
Gave mom or dad a hug		
Said "thank you"		
Said "please" when asking for something		
Initiated saying "hi"		
Put trash in the can		
Put on own seat belt		
Sat in chair without tipping it		
Put back pack away		

3. Develop a task analysis of a NCR 15-minute schedule.

Chapter 11

Extinction and Differential Reinforcement Procedures to Reduce Problem Behavior

GOALS

1. Define and Illustrate:
    a. Extinction
    b. Extinction burst
    c. DR
    d. DRA
    e. DRI
    f. DRD
    g. DRL
    h. DRO
2. Describe how to minimize the occurrence of extinction bursts.
3. Describe why positive behavior interventions are so important.

4. Complete this chapter's exercises/activities, or those assigned by your instructor.

*****

We discussed various strategies of preventing the occurrence of problem behavior in the previous chapter by changing what happens before the problem behavior. Now we turn our attention to reducing problem behaviors after they do occur using extinction and various differential reinforcement procedures (i.e., what happens after the behavior occurs).

EXTINCTION

Extinction involves *withholding or blocking whatever reinforcers are supporting the unwanted behavior of concern.* For a behavior to continue, it must be reinforced. If it is not, it withers and dies. The task of extinction is twofold. First you must identify what the reinforcers are for the behavior targeted for reduction. You learned to identify reinforcers in Chapter 6. You also learned that behavior tends to be maintained by attention, access to items or activities, escape, or sensory stimuli. So you must determine if the behavior targeted for reduction occurs because of the attention, escape, access and/or the sensory stimulation it provides your client. Once you determine the source or combination of these sources that maintain the behavior, your task is making sure that these reinforcers no longer occur following the targeted behavior. For example, some children tantrum to gain attention. "Misbehavior" often demands our attention, while good behavior does not. Even negative attention is better than no attention for many children. The parents are busy, and the child has learned that a tantrum works to gain their attention. So extinction in this situation would entail making sure no one gives the child attention for tantruming. Let's look at some illustrations:

Illustration 1: The mother is on the phone or talking to a friend in person. Your client calls out for mom. She ignores the child and continues talking to her friend. Your client starts yelling and screaming. The mother stops her conversation and asks him, "What is it?"

Let's do an A-B-C analysis of the above illustration:

A	B	C
Child calls. mother and she does not respond.	Child yells and screams.	Mother stops her conversation and says "What is it?" (She has given *attention* following yellintg and screaming.)

What did the child learn in this example? He learned that if mom does not respond initially, yell and scream to get her attention. The yelling and screaming worked to attain her attention.

What might you suggest the parent do? Here are several suggestions:

1. Teach the child how to obtain mom's attention in more constructive ways. (This is using DRA, a differential reinforcement procedure discussed below where you reinforce acceptable alternative behavior while you place the problem behavior on extinction.) For example, it might be helpful to teach your client to squeeze mom's hand or tap her on the shoulder twice when wanting to talk to her rather than yelling or having a tantrum. A wink, a nod, or a squeeze back can communicate, "I know you want to talk to me and I will make time to talk to you shortly." Of course, it is important that mother follow through and provide her child the time.

2. Help the mother schedule interactive times (she can set a timer for herself if needed) so the child can gain attention appropriately. This strategy also involves increasing the reinforcing nature of the environment as discusses in the previous chapter.

3. Teach the child to wait by reinforcing gradually longer periods of time that the child waits.

4. Withhold all reinforcers following each tantrum (i.e., use extinction). In other words, do not provide attention following the tantrum. In fact, it usually is best to withhold attention whenever a tantrum occurs to help ensure that the tantrum does not produce any type of reinforcement (attention, escape from a dreaded activity, or access to a desired item or activity).

Illustration 2: Your client, Susan, has been invited to a birthday party. Her mother takes her shopping in a toy store for the present. Susan sees a toy that she wants. Her mother tells her, "No, we are looking for a present for your friend." Susan starts to cry and stomp her feet. Mom tells her to be quiet, but she yells louder, and people in the store start looking at her. The mother then gives her the toy so she will be quiet and to avoid the embarrassment of the situation.

Let's do an A-B-C analysis of Susan's behavior:

A	B	C
Susan's mother tells her she can't have a toy she wants.	Susan starts crying and stomping her feet.	Susan's mother tells her to be quiet.
Susan's mother tells her to be quiet when she is crying and stomping her feet.	Susan yells louder.	Her mother gives her the toy she wants. (Susan gains *access* to the toy.)

What is Susan learning? Susan is learning that if she tantrums loud and long enough she is likely to get what she wants. In this case she was given the toy as a consequence of her temper tantrum. Thus, a tantrum is likely to occur whenever she does not immediately gain *access* to what she wants because the she has learned: "If I tantrum I'm likely to get what I want."

Let's also look at the mother's behavior. By letting Susan have or do what she wanted, the mother was able to stop the tantrum. When the tantrum stopped, she experienced relief, or negative reinforcement, by letting Susan have access to what she wanted. However, her tantrums will continue and possibly escalate over time. In other words, though the mother's short-term consequence was relief, her long-term consequence for letting Susan have what she wanted as a result of the tantrum is very punishing: an increase in tantrums to get what she wants.

What might you suggest the mother do in this type of situation? Here are several suggestions.

1. *Do not allow the tantrum to result in access to the activity or item* (i.e., use extinction). In other words, do not let her have the toy (the reinforcer). Another child started to tantrum in the grocery store because he wanted his mother to buy him some candy and she refused. Rather than giving him the candy, she picked up her son, left her groceries in the shopping cart, went to the car and waited until he calmed down before re-entering the store. (Another parent drove home rather than waiting.) She did not speak again to her son until he had been quiet for at least 3 minutes. In other situations, like at home, you and the parent can often wait out the tantrum. The main thing, as mentioned, is, *do not reinforce the tantrum* by giving Susan what she is seeking.

2. *Teach how to behave*. Discuss the shopping trip with Susan before going and inform her that, if she can help her mother select something for her friend and not ask for something for herself, the two of them can go get ice cream (or do something special) after they are done shopping. And then, of course, provide the promised activity after the shopping if Susan did not ask for something for herself. (This involves two differential reinforcement procedures described below, a DRA in that she gets reinforced for helping mom find a gift for her friend rather than engaging in a tantrum, and a DRO where she gets reinforced for no tantrums.)

Illustration 3: Michelle refuses to do her homework and starts screaming when her mother asks her to do it. She sends Michelle to her room for 30 minutes as punishment. While in her room Michelle watches TV, plays with toys, or plays games on her computer—all things she loves to do.

Let's do an A-B-C analysis on Michelle's behavior:

A	B	C
Michele is told to do her homework.	Michele refuses and starts screaming.	Michele is sent to her room where she doesn't have to do her homework (excapes homework) and she plays with her toys and computer.

This is a common mistake that many parents make. They remove their demand and/or change the requested activity (i.e., redirect—see Chapter 10) so that their child is likely to stop the tantrum and so the parents can receive negative reinforcement (i.e. removal of tantrum). But what is actually happening to Michelle's screaming? It is NOT being punished. Doing homework is most likely an aversive activity for Michelle. So, she is learning that screaming gets her out of doing her homework. In other words the tantrum works for the child. The tantrum provides an *escape* from the dreaded task or activity. Next time the child wants to *escape* from a task or activity, he/she is likely to tantrum because it has worked in the past (she has received negative reinforcement for engaging in tantrums). So, when the purpose of the child's behavior is to escape from the previous activity, you will need to help the mother avoid removing her demands, or using re-direction to a new activity.

What can the mother do in place of removing the task? There are several possibilities:

1. *It is critical that the tantrum does not result in removal of the task or activity that the child wants to avoid doing (i.e., implement extinction conditions for the tantrum).* Thus, make it clear to the child from the start that if she tantrums, all privileges (playing with friends, television, computer, iPad, etc.) will be removed until at least some of the task is performed. If your child needs

help performing the task due to its difficulty, provide assistance, but do not do the task for the child.
2. Once the child has done some of the task (with your help if necessary), you can then switch to another activity if it seems appropriate. This way the escape from the dreaded activity (negative reinforcement) follows some work on it, rather than following the tantrum. The reinforcer of escape is withheld or blocked (extinction).

In addition to the above, you can try several other interventions, and help the caregiver implement those that prove effective. As you will recognize, some of these are from Chapter 10.

- Reduce the task demands before the misbehavior starts and then gradually increase them over time.
- Avoid presenting the entire task or assignment at once. Instead, cover up some of the assignment before the tantrum or other misbehavior occurs, and just focus on getting each part done.
- Provide praise and other reinforcers for compliance (DRA—see below).
- Teach your client how to appropriately request a break or help (use DRA, modeling, and provide role-playing or reinforced practice).
- Provide recognition for doing the work (DRA), and for the absence of whining, crying, or complaining (DRO—see below).

A note of caution. When you first begin to use extinction by denying access, escape, and/or attention following a tantrum (or most any problem behaviors), your client is likely to engage in the problem behavior more loudly and more intensely. This initial increase in intensity of the problem behaviors, along with perhaps aggression and crying, is called an extinction burst. After all, the tantrum worked in the past for the client, so, when the client finds that it is not working, the first reaction will be to increase its severity. *You will need to anticipate this temporary increase in severity and continue to hold fast to not providing any of the reinforcer(s)* (i.e., the escape, access, and/or attention).

Eventually, the tantrums will decrease once the youngster realizes that they no longer work.

Consistency is very important. If you or another (e.g., parent or teacher) withhold escape, access and/or attention some of the time, but not at other times, the misbehavior is likely to become well established and more difficult to eliminate in that person's presence. Your client learns that "it may not work all the time, but if I do it again and again, it might work." If you and the parents are consistent, the child is more likely eventually to stop the behavior after a period of initial testing.

Also note that in each illustration above, we combined extinction with a differential reinforcement procedure. This is critical because research has shown differential reinforcement reduces or eliminates extinction bursts and your client's resistance to extinction. In other words, the problem behavior is less likely to increase in severity and last for a shorter period of time when differential reinforcement is part of the extinction intervention. Thus, we will now discuss differential reinforcement.

DIFFERENTIAL REINFORCEMENT (DR)

DR *involves reinforcing a behavior when it occurs under specific conditions and not others* (to help the client discriminate when and when not to engage in the behavior) *or when we reinforce a specific behavior(s) under certain conditions but not other behaviors.* There are several types of differential reinforcement procedures that go by various acronyms. The one we address below are: DRA, DRD, DRL, and DRO.

DRA, or Differential Reinforcement of Alternative Behaviors

DRA *involves reinforcing alternative responses to the problem behavior, while placing the problem behavior on extinction or using some other procedure to reduce the problem behavior.* Too often we find ourselves saying: "Stop that"; "Don't"; and, "Be quiet." These responses to problem behavior take no thought and become an automatic reaction on our part. Teaching the child how to behave, however, does require some thought, planning, and effort on our part. We have to determine what we want our child to do in place of the problem behavior. We have to request it and perhaps explain and model it. And we always have to reinforce its occurrence while at the same time withholding any reinforcement to the problem behavior (extinction). *The DRA intervention helps teach your clients what to do to get what they want in a more productive way.*

The "catch them being good" chart in Chapter 10 can be used to help increase the use of DRA in the home. Let's look at some other illustrations.

Illustrations of DRA

Problem: Child yells for your attention.

Intervention: Withhold your attention for yelling and only give your attention when your child asks for your attention appropriately (e.g., taps your shoulder, asks in a polite, normal tone of voice, or whatever works for your situation). To help your client learn this alternative behavior, you probably will have to go through the steps listed above—request, explain and/or model it, and reinforce appropriate requesting. It is important to remember never to request or explain what to do right after they have engaged in problem behavior. Learning appropriate strategies to gain attention (or escape) needs to happen before the problem behavior not afterward, or later when the client is engaged in appropriate behavior.

Problem: Child frequently does not do chores or homework.

Intervention: Provide reinforcement, including having friends over, going out to play, using the iPad, etc., *only* after chores and/or homework are completed. Privileges, or reinforcers, are only permitted after completion. Your client can chose not to do chores and/or homework, but loses all privileges until they are completed.

Problem: Child demands lunch.

Intervention: Withhold attention from demanding. Reinforce polite asking (e.g., "Mom, I'm really hungry. Can you please fix me some lunch?") You will need to help the parent teach polite asking by having the parent model, request, and differentially reinforce polite asking. As the client begins to become proficient in polite asking, the requesting and modeling prompts can be faded.

DRI, or Differential Reinforcement of Incompatible Behavior

DRI *"is a sub-class of DRA, with a further restriction: the alternative behavior cannot be emitted simultaneously with the unwanted behavior"* (Mayer et al., 2014, p. 577) . For example, the goal is to have your client remain in his seat while doing his work. To use DRI, you would reinforce in-seat behavior and not reinforce out-of-seat behavior. If you provide reinforcement to the client for tapping his mother on the shoulder to gain her attention, and withhold reinforcement for yelling, you would be using DRA in that the client could also yell while tapping mom on the shoulder. Thus, to be a DRI, a special case of DRA, the undesired behavior must not be able to occur at the same time as the behavior you are reinforcing. For example, one of the authors was working with a teenage boy who was aggressive in the halls when changing classes. A DRI was set up to eliminate this behavior. He would earn reinforcement for keeping his hands in his pockets, because it was incompatible with hitting others during transition time.

DRD, or Differential Reinforcement of Diminishing Rates

DRD *involves providing reinforcement when the rate of the behavior is equal to or less than a specified limit.* In other words you are reinforcing improvement or fewer infractions per a unit of time. This positive intervention recognizes that change takes time; it does not occur immediately. To implement this procedure you provide reinforcement when the infraction (e.g., noncompliance or tantrums) has not occurred as frequently as it did in the past. In other words, your client has made some improvement. After success at one level (your client is now engaging in fewer infractions), gradually decrease the number of infractions that must occur in that time period for your client to receive reinforcement. Let us look at some examples to help clarify its use.

Illustrations of DRD

   Problem: Temper tantrums.

Intervention: Maria typically has three tantrums during the day. Today, she only had two. This improvement is pointed out and she is provided with praise for only having two. After she has been able to maintain this reduction in her tantrums for two or three days, the praise occurs only if there is no more than one tantrum. The reinforcement continues to be delivered for fewer and fewer occurrence over time (e.g., no more than one in two days, one in three days, one a week, etc., for the reinforcement, or praise to be provided.)

Problem: Noncompliance

Intervention: Terry typically refuses to do what her father requests an average of four times in the morning. Any morning that the noncompliance occurs only three times or less, reinforcement is provided by Terry's father. Once this has occurred for at least two consecutive days, reinforcement is provided after only two times, etc.

This intervention has the advantage that it is tolerable and can reduce infractions without the use of punishment. However, it does not teach new ways of behaving. Therefore, combine its application with modeling and reinforcing appropriate alternative behavior (DRA) that can help the child get what she wants without the tantrum. This might include asking for a break in place of having a tantrum to get out of an unpleasant activity, or waiting rather than having to have an item now, or asking for help to gain attention rather than having a tantrum. By combining the interventions, it provides more reinforcement, an important outcome as pointed out in Chapter 10.

DRL, or Differential Reinforcement of Lower Rates

DRL *involves providing reinforcement for the problem behavior after a pre-specified period of time goes by in which it has not occurred.* In our opinion its use in applied settings, such as the home or school, is limited to desired behaviors that are a problem because they occur to an excessive degree. So, you need to reduce them, but do not want to eliminate them. For example, you want your client to participate in discussion at home and school, but your client dominates the discussions, not allowing others sufficient time to participate in a meaningful manner. In such a situation you might use a DRL in which you would reinforce participation only after a specified period of non-participation has occurred to allow others to participate. Or, rather than requiring an amount of time to pass before your client participates again, you could set the contingency up so that at least one or two others have participated before you recognize or reinforce your client's participation again. In other words, we recommend that you restrict the use of this procedure to acceptable behaviors that occur too frequently or rapidly.

DRO, or Differential Reinforcement of Other Behavior, or Differential Reinforcement of Zero Occurrence, or Omission Training

DRO goes by several names in the literature. We prefer the term Differential Reinforcement of Zero Occurrence because when you use DRO you *provide reinforcement only when the behavior did not occur*. Further, even though other behaviors are likely occurring when the reinforcement is provided, no particular behavior reliably receives reinforcers. Therefore, any particular acts are unlikely to increase very much, if at all (Mayer, et al., 2014, p. 582).

DRO, then, *involves providing reinforcement after the behavior has not or is not occurring*. For example, you might look up at predetermined times to see whether or not there is a finger in your client's mouth. Provide reinforcement to your client by confirming and pointing out that there is not a finger in her/his mouth. Or, for your client to receive reinforcement, no finger must touch the mouth for at least 15 minutes. Other examples are provided below.

Illustrations of DRO

Problem: Noncompliance
Intervention: As long as noncompliance has not occurred during the morning routine, reinforcement is provided.

Problem: Tantrums
Intervention: Reinforcement is provided if no tantrums occur during any two-hour block of time in which your client is awake. Once two consecutive 2-hour blocks occur without tantrums for 2 consecutive days, the time is increased to 3 hours without tantrums for the

reinforcement. This increase of the time interval continues to gradually increase until tantrums no longer occur, or are at an acceptable level.

Problem: Self-stimulation (e.g., weaving head, flapping hands)
Intervention: Reinforce for gradually longer periods in which the problem behavior does not occur.

Caution—Reinforcing for non-occurrence, like with the previous intervention, does not teach your client what to do. It also focuses your attention on infractions, rather than on appropriate behavior. Thus, it is best to combine it with modeling and reinforcement of acceptable alternative behaviors. It also can be combined with reinforcing diminishing rates. For example, Song's tantrums occur to escape from tasks that she dislikes. We can model and reinforce her asking for a break and asking for help (acceptable alternative behaviors). We also can provide reinforcement for *fewer tantrums* throughout the day, and we can provide reinforcement for the *absence of tantrums* for every two hours. By combining all four, we are able to reinforce more frequently, likely resulting in a more rapid reduction in tantrums without involving punishment.

SUMMARY AND CONCLUSIONS

Tantrums and many other problem behaviors can be prevented or reduced by using the interventions described in this and the previous chapter. In particular it is important that you:

1. Provide a positive, reinforcing environment to help foster pro-social, productive behaviors and to prevent problem behaviors.
2. Recognize that what works for one child may not work for another in that each child's personality is as unique as his or her fingerprints. Thus, identify reinforcers and appropriate interventions for *your* client.
3. Use an ABC chart to learn more about what might be accidentally reinforcing problem behavior.

4. Always teach your client alternative, acceptable behaviors for escaping demands, obtaining access to activities or items, and gaining attention.
5. Avoid the common mistake of removing your demand, or providing escape (e.g., timeout), from the requested activity to help stop the tantrum or other misbehavior.
6. Avoid the common mistake of providing an activity or item desired by the child to help stop the tantrum.
7. Avoid the common mistake of giving attention to disruptions or tantrums when that is what your child is trying to obtain by the tantrums.
8. Be prepared to experience a transitory increase in the tantrums' intensity and duration when you start your intervention, particularly if it has been occurring for a while.
9. Create a positive behavior chart.
10. Use modeling and reinforce desired alternative behaviors to help teach your client how to behave appropriately.
11. Reinforce the nonoccurrence and/or lower rates of problem behavior in combination with modeling and reinforcing alternative behaviors.

We hope the material presented in this chapter will help you to improve your clients' behavior and your relationship with your client. These positive behavior interventions should be used on most infractions. When their use is based on a functional behavior assessment, they appear to be every bit as effective as punishment, and do not have the negative side effects of punishment. Plus, the more of these you can combine in your intervention (as suggested in #11 above), the more rapid a behavioral change you can achieve. Additional research supporting many of the suggested interventions and more in-depth discussions of these topics can be found in Chapters 26–28 of the textbook by Mayer et al. (2014).

EXERCISES

After you have completed the exercises below, you will want feedback. Your instructor has access (or can obtain access from the publisher) to sample answers for each of the following exercises:

1. List the factors that influence how rapidly a behavior is reduced through extinction.
2. Karla commented, "I was so surprised. I started to ignore little Jimmy when he talked in a silly voice and he came up and hit me. I never recalled that before." (a) Explain to Karla why Jimmy's reaction is not surprising. (b) State what can be done to help minimize these types of side effects.
3. Differentiate between DRL and DRO.
4. Your client's behavior plan states that you will use a DRO 5-minute schedule for tantrums. When will you provide reinforcement to your client? What will you do if during those five minutes your client engages in problem behavior?
5. Try and come up with possible incompatible behaviors for the following problem behavior to use in a DRI procedure: (1) Thumbsucking (2) Hitting (3) Leaning back in chair (4) throwing toys."

ACTIVITIES

1. Use modeling and reinforcing desired alternative behaviors to help teach yourself, or someone else (only under the supervision of a BCBA), how to behave. Identify the problem and alternative behaviors. Describe how you are using modeling and DRA. If possible, check you answer with your BCBA or fellow students.
2. Identify a problem behavior and describe how you might reinforce the non-occurrence and/or lower rates of problem behavior. Combine this with modeling and reinforcing alternative behaviors, along with other interventions described in previous chapters (that you have tailored to yourself or friend) to help reduce a problem behavior. Be sure to identify the behavior and each procedure you are using. If possible, check your answer with your BCBA or fellow students.

Chapter 12

Punishment and Crisis Management

GOALS

1. Define and give examples of punishment.
2. List at least five negative side effects of punishment.
3. Define negative punishment, response cost, bonus response cost, and timeout.
4. Illustrate response cost.
5. List at least four things that you can do to help reduce the side effects of response cost.
6. Define timeout.
7. Give at least three different examples of inclusion timeout.
8. Give at least three different examples of exclusionary timeout and explain how it is different from seclusion timeout.
9. Describe how to use negative punishment effectively.

10. Define positive punishment, and illustrate and describe how it differs from negative punishment.
11. Define and illustrate negative practice.
12. Define and illustrate overcorrection, including positive practice and restitution.
13. Point out the dangers of using corporal punishment.
14. Define what constitutes a crisis situation.
15. Explain what the purpose is of a Crisis Management protocol.
16. Discuss how you might be able to break the chain of events leading to a crisis situation.
17. Complete this chapter's exercises/activities, or those assigned by your instructor.

*****

SHOULD I USE A PUNITIVE CONSEQUENCE TO STOP CHALLENGING BEHAVIOR?

This is not an easy question to answer. Despite its connotations, punishment is not inherently evil. It happens to all of us. We might turn the wrong knob in the shower, touch a hot stove, get a ticket for speeding or running a red light, engage in a penalty and have yardage taken away in a football game, or be given the "cold shoulder" from a close friend or spouse. Punishment is a fact of nature; it is an on-going part of life. It helps to teach us what not to do. **Punishment**, as pointed out in Chapter 3, *is any consequence that decreases the future likelihood of the behavior*. We need to understand it if we are going to be maximally effective in working with our clients. Before we start using punishment, it is really important to understand and acknowledge that the use of punishment can be associated with some unwanted side effects.

In fact, punishment can have a number of *negative side effects*. These include: violence or aggression toward others or the facilities (vandalism or property damage), escape (e.g., at home this can be leaving a specific area, or the house; at school it can be leaving a specific area, being tardy, cutting class, being truant, dropping out), lowered reported image of self, and suppression of appropriate behaviors (not just the one being punished). Clients also can habituate to aversive stimuli if they are frequently used as behavior control methods. This habituation refers to the client "getting used" to the aversive stimuli. As a result, the aversive stimuli lose their effectiveness in reducing the behavior. This tends to occur when the aversive stimuli are frequently used on a behavior, or used on a variety of behaviors. Such habituation often results in more intense or severe punishment being needed to have the same effect, and this usually increases the intensity and frequency of the negative side effects. In addition to these negative side effects, remember, punishment does not teach what to do—just what not to do.

Punishment, then, must be selected for use with caution. *Be sure not to use it until you know the function(s) of the infraction, have tried or ruled out positive behavior interventions, and have obtained the approval of your BCBA and the client's guardians.* To avoid its overuse, resulting in habituation and other negative side effects, *punishment should only be used with behaviors that are severe. By severe, we mean behaviors that place the client or others in danger or are so disruptive they cannot be tolerated (i.e., behavior that is more than just annoying).* Also, be sure to combine punishment with DRA and other more constructive alternatives to punishment to help teach your client, not just how not to behave, but also *how to* behave correctly. By doing so, you will help reduce the negative side effects of punishment. Keeping these points in mind, let's look at several punitive procedures that are often used in homes and schools. We will start with two **negative punishment** procedures, or procedures that contingently *reduce the infraction by reducing or denying access to positive reinforcers as the consequence of an act.*

NEGATIVE PUNISHMENT

Response Cost

We have all experienced response cost. When using **response cost** you remove or *take away a certain amount of reinforcers from the client* *contingent on the infraction.* For example, money is taken away when a traffic ticket is given. Yards may be taken away as a result of a penalty in football. Parents may contingently take away points earned in a token economy, part of an allowance, television time, or playtime. Response cost is often referred to as "fines."

To help reduce the negative side effects we mentioned above, there are several things you can do:

- Return half the fine if the child immediately gets back to work, or he returns to the activity in which he was involved or asked to do.
- Keep fines minimal. You do not want your client winding up in "debtors' prison," but be careful not to gradually increase the fine either (remember we just talked briefly about habituation—if you gradually increase the fine it will not be effective). You must choose a fine that is just right—not too high, but not too low either. Moreover, you have to match or exceed the penalty that the client has recently experienced, or the procedure is not likely to reduce the behavior. That is, if your client is used to being fined four points for hitting, and you decide to fine two points for hitting, the two points are not likely to work. You will need to fine four to six points to make it work. Thus, it is best to set appropriate fines from the onset.
- Combine with identifying appropriate behaviors for which your clients can earn points. *Earning points should always exceed losing points* (i. e., a response cost procedure should be combined with a token economy or some other way of earning points for appropriate behaviors).
- Some prefer to use what is called "Bonus Response Cost" to help reduce the negative side effects. **Bonus response cost** *involves taking away points or tokens from a pool of bonus reinforcers that the client has not earned*, and works best when used in conjunction with a token economy, or a similar program for earning points for appropriate behavior. For example, the parent, RBT, or teacher might set up the program to have ten bonus points or tokens. If the client engages in the serious infraction, a set number (e.g., 4) are removed from the bonus pool. The client receives the number of bonus points or tokens left at the end of the ses-

sion. This way, the token or points that the client has earned are not being removed, and the client receives bonus points for the absence, or low occurrence, of the serious infraction.
- Combine with DRA or DRI, and/or modeling, to help teach the client how to behave.

In one of the author's homes, kids earn "family bucks" for doing homework, getting ready for school in the morning, independently doing their bedtime routine, and doing various chores around the house. In addition to earning "family bucks" for engaging in these various appropriate behaviors, they can also lose "family bucks" for engaging in serious infractions including: hitting someone, talking back to mom, or getting in trouble at school.

Timeout

Timeout also is a procedure most all of us have experienced and/or used. **Timeout** involves *removing access to reinforcers, contingent on the occurrence of the severe infraction, for a short period of time* (two to five minutes; *yes you read that right, effective timeout will not be longer than five minutes)*. There are several levels of timeout with increasing severity. It is best to use the least severe form of timeout that works.

Inclusion timeout. Inclusion timeout is *the least intrusive/aversive form of timeout and the most commonly used. It involves restricting the client from participating in the ongoing activities due to his or her misbehavior. The client may hear and see what is going on, but cannot participate or be responded to by others when inclusion timeout is in effect.* There are four common examples of inclusion timeout:

Timeout ribbon—This relatively benign form of timeout is used with groups, but can be modified to use with an individual. A ribbon is placed around the neck of each participant like a necktie. If one of the participants engages in one of the identified serious infractions (e.g., hitting, pushing, kicking, etc.) the ribbon is removed from around his or her neck. An individual without a ribbon can see and hear what is going on but no one responds to that person, nor is that person allowed to participate in the activity that the others are involved in for two to five minutes (depending on what is likely to work). After the two to five minutes, the ribbon is returned and the person can again gain access to the activity and interactions.

Planned ignoring—Here, all attention (physical contact and interaction) is removed contingent upon the serious infraction. The RBT or others remove any reinforcing material in front of them, and they turn their backs and do not respond to the client for the brief timeout period that is contingent upon the occurrence of the problem behavior. Once the preset timeout period is over, the RBT turns around contingent upon the client's engagement in appropriate behavior, rather than the problem behavior, and the RBT attempts to engage the client again. Remember that with punishment, it is always necessary to make sure you are also reinforcing appropriate behavior.

No, planned ignoring is not extinction—You will recall that extinction involves withholding reinforcement to a behavior, while other behaviors are eligible for reinforcement. Here, no behavior is eligible for reinforcement until the timeout period is completed. Also, remember that extinction depends on the function of the behavior, which may not always be to gain attention. Planned ignoring is not a good strategy to use if your client frequently elopes, because elopement might occur while your back is turned.

Withdrawal of materials—This variation of timeout is similar to planned ignoring. All reinforcing materials, such as toys, games, and electronic devices are removed, along with ignoring the client's behaviors for a brief period of time. Your back is not turned on the client, but no attention is given. Once the timeout period is over, and the client has engaged in appropriate behavior, the materials can be returned to the individual.

Contingent observation—Relocate your client, contingent upon the infraction, to an area where he or she can see and hear what is going on but is not allowed to participate. This inclusion timeout is frequently used in various competitive sports where the player must sit on the bench and watch what is going on contingent on a rule violation. Another example would be removing the client from the swimming pool contingent on a serious infraction, and having him or her watch but not participate for the preset timeout period. In a recent personal example, one of the authors used contingent observation with her son when her son hit another child at a Disneyland playground. The author removed her son from the center of the playground, moved him to the outskirts of the playground, and withheld all attention for two minutes.

You must be very cautious in using timeout. Timeout will only work if the environment from which you are removing access is reinforcing. In other words, timeout only works if "time in" is desired. The previous example with one of the authors' son shows that if Disneyland were not so fun, removing her son to the sideline would not have been effective. Moreover, if it is a punitive environment (your client is doing math and hates it, or has had a lot of failure experiences with it), and you remove the client from doing his math contingent on the infraction, you are not using timeout. You are using negative reinforcement in that the client is learning if he engages in the infraction, he can escape the punitive environment. In other words, your attempt to stop the infraction is in reality teaching the client to misbehave to escape from the punitive activity. *Do not apply timeout for escape-motivated behavior.* Also, do not use for automatic or self-reinforcing behaviors, in that the client likely will use the timeout period to self-stimulate (e.g., if the client engages in hand flapping and it is maintained by automatic reinforcement, and you place the individual in "timeout," the client will likely engage in hand flapping the whole time). For timeout to work, access to reinforcement must be denied, not provided by providing escape. (Remember that a functional behavioral assessment needs to be conducted prior to applying most any punitive procedure.)

Exclusionary timeout—To use this variety of timeout you either *place your client in a non-reinforcing environment or remove the reinforcing environment from the client contingent on the infraction.* Exclusion timeout is different from inclusion timeout in that your client is not only denied access to reinforcers, but also cannot observe and/or hear what others are doing for a brief period of time (e.g., your client is sitting in the hall facing the wall away from others). The ethical practice of this form of timeout prohibits physically blocking or locking a client in the non-reinforcing environment. The key to its effectiveness is providing a non-reinforcing timeout environment, while ensuring the *time in* environment is reinforcing. If the client's bedroom is full of toys, television, computer, and other electronic devices your client frequently uses, the bedroom should not be used as a timeout room. Instead, you might have your client sit at the end of a hallway or some location you, the parents, or the teacher determine as non-reinforcing. Sometimes it is possible to remove the reinforcing environment from the client. For example, if your client screams, kicks, and hits when he does not get a cookie or other requested items, you or the parent can leave the area with the cookies, close the door behind you, and leave the child and tantrum in the kitchen. (While out of the kitchen, hide the cookies.)

Other forms of timeout—Other forms of timeout include *seclusion timeout*, which is the removal of a client to a specific location contingent on problem behavior, and *restrained timeout*, where the client is restrained contingent on problem behavior. It has been our experience that more severe forms of timeout, such as seclusion (e.g., using a special locked or unlocked timeout room) and restrained timeout usually are not necessary as long as you rely heavily on the reinforcement-based behavior reduction procedures, such as DRA, modeling and others we have previously discussed in Chapters 10 and 11.

Effective Use of Negative Punishment

Several suggestions have been provided to minimize the negative side effects of response cost. Related to those, the following points apply to both response cost and timeout. When using negative punishment, it is important to:

- Keep the fines minimal and durations of timeout short (two to about five minutes). Many clients find ways of making the timeout environment somewhat reinforcing if left in timeout too long. Also, as you know, longer timeouts tend to make shorter timeouts ineffective. Remember timeout works because time in is reinforcing. After five minutes the client starts to "forget" how reinforcing time in was, thus making timeout not so bad.

- Apply the response cost, or timeout, *immediately following each time* the major infraction occurs. Think about this for a minute: speeding fines are designed to reduce speeding. Some people still speed after they have received a ticket. Why? Because they do not get a ticket every time they speed. Imagine if your car sent a signal to the Department of Motor Vehicles and you got a ticket each time you were speeding—would you speed? We think not.
- Be sure to avoid discussing the procedure or infraction with the child during timeout or right after the infraction. This could provide reinforcing attention. Discussions of the punishment should occur *before* any problems occur or *after* the child has been fined or completed the timeout and is engaged in appropriate behavior. It is always best to clearly delineate the consequences in advance. "If you do _____, you will have to go into timeout."
- Keep the number of behaviors you use timeout or response cost on to no more than about three to avoid overuse, making the environment too aversive, and to help avoid the procedure becoming less effective due to overuse. Remember, these procedures are for intolerable behaviors only: behaviors that represent a danger to others or the client.
- Find out what timeout periods or fines have been used. If the fines involved many points, or the timeout periods were long (greater than 10 minutes), we advise against the use of the response cost or timeout procedure. As you recall, the procedure must match or exceed what has been used for it to be effective. You do not want to create such a highly punitive environment. (You can try stopping the procedures for about two months, and then try the shorter periods to see if they will work.)
- Decide with the BCBA and parent or teacher if it is a good idea to add the contingency that the child must be quiet for at least 30 seconds before being allowed out of timeout.
- Allow shorter timeouts if the client goes to timeout without resistance and is quiet during the timeout period. For example, a four-minute timeout could be reduced to two minutes. Similarly, half the fine could be returned if the client immediately gets back

to work after being fined or accepts the fine without aggressing further.

- *Always provide reinforcement of alternative behaviors at times other than when the timeout period is in effect to help your client discriminate the behavior that is not acceptable.* Giving clients treats and praise when they are displaying appropriate behavior and using timeout as a consequence for the occurrence of a problem behavior will help them discriminate correct from incorrect behavior.
- *Do not overuse*. Both response cost and timeout are often overused. Why? Because the person using the procedure often receives immediate reinforcement for its use, and/or because the problem behavior tends to be rapidly reduced (negative reinforcement). Thus, be very cautious that you or those you are working with don't start over using the procedure because of the reinforcement it provides you. (We all seek relief from aversive situations.)

POSITIVE PUNISHMENT

Positive punishment involves *adding an aversive consequence following the infraction,* rather than taking away or denying access to reinforcers (negative punishment), *that reduces the future occurrence of the infraction.* There are numerous forms of punishment that are used for various behavior issues. Positive punishment is often used to correct an error made by a client (e.g., "No, this is the correct way"—where "No" is a conditioned punisher). Examples of positive punishment are when: one touches a hot stove (the burn is the punisher that discourages touching it again in the future), gets in a shower before the temperature is adjusted (again, the burn, or cold, is the punisher), gets an item incorrect on a test or at work (the disparaging feedback is the punisher that discourages getting an item incorrect in the future), gets in an accident while texting (the accident is the punisher that discourages texting while driving in the future), or is yelled at (the aversive social feedback is the punisher that discourages the behavior that got yelled at in the future). It is being used when one verbally disapproves of an action another takes, or when a coach has his students run around the track or do push ups as a result of an infraction.

Punishers are as unique and individual as reinforcers. What is a punitive consequence for one client may not be for another. Therefore, in all these examples, the consequence is considered punishing only if it reduces the future occurrences of the behavior it follows. There are also a number of positive punishment variations. The more common ones are described below.

Negative Practice

Sometimes parents or teachers use what is called **negative practice**, a form of positive punishment in which the child is *required to practice the unwanted behavior repeatedly for a predetermined time following each occurrence of the infraction*. For example, the child is caught smoking by the parent. The parent has the child smoke several cigarettes in a row until smoking becomes aversive or a punishing experience for the child. A student writes a profane word on his paper. The teacher has him write it 100 times. This is not a procedure we recommend, because we don't want the person to practice the inappropriate behavior. We would rather the client practices an appropriate behavior (*positive practice*) than engage in the unwanted behavior repeatedly.

Overcorrection

Overcorrection is another positive punishment procedure that we have used at times. **Overcorrection** *involves two components*: **restitution**, *restoring or repairing the environmental destruction or disruption to an improved state*, and **positive practice**, *repeatedly practicing a positive alternative behavior contingent upon the infraction*. Use only the second if the first does not apply. Overcorrection is often considered educative in that the child learns what effort it takes to restore the environment back to it original state (or slightly improved state), plus they learn an alternative behavior. For example, if the client makes a mark on the wall, the client must clean off the mark, plus another part of the wall (restitution), and repeatedly make marks on a piece of paper (positive practice—the client is taught where it is OK to make marks). Another time one of the authors used positive punishment was with a client who would hand-flap. Each time he flapped his hands he was required to hold them up above his head for three seconds, straight out to his side for three seconds, straight out in front of him for three seconds, and down to his side for three seconds. This positive practice routine was repeated 10 times each time he hand-flapped in public. (Because there was no environmental damage or disruption, restitution was not used.) It was okay for him to hand-flap in his room or bathroom. He soon learned, after two to three months, not to flap his hands in public, only in his bedroom or bathroom. Allowing hand-flaps in specific environments without an aversive consequence and punishing the behavior in the inappropriate environments is using a positive reinforcement procedure (DRA) and a positive punishment procedure together. Blending the two procedures teaches the client where he is allowed to engage in the behavior and where is he is not.

Corporal Punishment

Corporal punishment, such as spankings, hitting, slapping, is a more severe form of positive punishment that we usually do not recommend because its frequent use has been shown to increase the likelihood of the following client outcomes:

- aggression
- delinquent and antisocial behavior
- risk of becoming a victim of physical abuse
- adult aggression
- risk of abusing one's own child or spouse,
- adult criminal and antisocial behavior,
- decreased quality of the relationship between parent and child,
- a decrease in the child's mental health
- decrease in adult mental health

Often we do not realize the damage corporal punishment is doing because we often do not see its effects until years later.

Any form of punishment, positive or negative, should not be used unless it is based on a functional behavior assessment, and data are collected to monitor its effects on your client's behavior. The intervention program must be modified or discontinued if the data show it to be ineffective or no longer needed. Also it is most important that you combine intervention with DRA and other forms of differential reinforcement. By doing so, you not only reduce the negative side effects of punishment, but you also focus more on teaching your client acceptable ways of behaving and help make the client's environment more positive, less aversive. It also is important to recognize that positive punishment permeates our society and is often used more frequently in the home and classroom than praise or positive recognition—a situation that needs to be reversed.

CRISIS MANAGEMENT

My client is going to hurt himself or herself or someone else, what should I do?

If you are working with an individual whose problem behavior can pose a serious risk to themselves or to others, a **Crisis Management** protocol must be included in the behavior plan. A crisis management protocol provides a step-by-step guide of how to deal with serious behavior that threatens to harm either the client, others, or property. Generally speaking, crises have three elements in common: 1) there is a threat to self, others, or property; 2) there is an element of surprise; 3) there is a short decision time. As such, it is important to have in writing how the crisis should be managed. The purpose of the protocol is to ensure that the RBT, parents, and teachers all stay calm, manage their own responses, set limits, prevent physical confrontations, and ensure safety. There are a number of companies (e.g., CPI, PCMA) that can be contracted to certify individuals in the use of crisis management techniques. Most programs equip staff with skills to prevent behaviors from occurring and ways to empower clients to manage their own behavior. Also, they should include specific control procedures to physically ensure everyone's safety. Like punishment procedures, untrained individuals should *never* implement crisis management techniques. Moreover, any crisis management protocol should be developed by a BCBA and approved by the team. Approval of all stakeholders must be obtained before implementing such procedures.

CPI has 10 tips to de-escalate crisis situations.

1. Be empathic. This means don't judge or discount other people's behavior or feelings. In fact, you should pay attention to them. Remember, what they are going through is very central to their lives and is important.
2. Respect Personal Space. Give the person some breathing room (e.g., 1.5 feet). Think about how you would feel if someone was invading your personal space or up in your face.
3. Watch your body language. Make sure you are non-threatening with your body language. This also includes gestures, facial expressions, and tone of voice.
4. Do *not* overreact. Ensure that you are not escalating the situation; remain calm, rational, and professional.
5. Be supportive. Point out what they must be feeling and let them know you are there to help them.
6. Do *not* engage in a power struggle. Don't get into a discussion at this time regarding the rights and wrong of the situation. It is important to ignore the challenge itself, but this does not mean ignore the person. Use redirection to get them back on track, rather than focusing on the issue.
7. Ensure limits are pre-established. Do not set limits on what constitutes a crisis in the moment, ensure limits are pre-set and pre-taught.
8. Pick your battles. If options or flexibility are available, offer them.
9. Remember, silence is golden. Sometimes everyone in the situation just needs a communication and commotion break (a break from all the stimulation). You don't have to "talk" your way through a crisis—remember, silence is sometimes golden. Try to limit commotion around the client and stop talking to them for a brief

time until they deescalate. For example, if Marty is agitated because of all the commotion in the work area (e.g., other clients and staff transitioning to other areas), you don't have to keep talking to him and telling him to calm down and that it will soon be over. In fact, in this instance, it would be best to prompt him once to calm down. Then be quiet, and ensure Marty and the others are safe. Let Marty get a break from all the noise, which includes you talking to him.

10. Allow some time to calm down. It is hard for anyone to calm down in half a second, so give them some time. Do not rush them to calm down; this can just escalate the situation.

The main thing to remember in a crisis situation is that your goal is to de-escalate the situation, ensuring the safety of everyone and the surroundings. We highly recommend being trained in one of the publicly available crisis management programs. In addition to being trained on de-escalation techniques and restraint procedures, it is important to understand the laws regarding restraints in the state in which you are practicing. In most states, individuals with developmental disabilities can only be restrained to control behaviors that create an emergency or a crisis situation. It is suggested that staff try every effort to avoid the use of restraint, and they should try to redirect and diffuse the situation before it reaches crisis magnitude. Most agencies and facilities have their own policy and procedures related to the use of restraints, so you should ask the your agency or facility for a copy of their policies.

The process of using restraints usually starts with a written policy on the use of restraints and permission to use the restraints within the behavioral plan. In addition to a policy, all staff must be trained to competency on all the procedures. Upon implementation of a restraint procedure, staff must immediately notify the highest-level direct care supervisor. Restraints should not last longer than an hour, but if they do, special approval must be obtained. Restraint must end when the emergency ends. In addition, the individuals who performed the restraints must immediately fill out an incident report and send it to the individuals' team. Never use restraints without prior approval of the client's guardians and your supervisors.

One other possible suggestion that may help diffuse a potential crisis situation: become aware that often a client will provide signals that they are about to have a tantrum or engage in dangerous behaviors. For example, a chain of events may occur, starting with a sigh, putting the head down, defiance, criticizing others, yelling, swearing, followed by physical aggression. The idea in these situations is to break the chain of events by redirecting the client early in the chain, such as when putting the head down. At that point, redirect the client to a desired activity, or start talking to the client about a topic that is a major interest to him or her.

SUMMARY AND CONCLUSIONS

Sometimes our best efforts for changing problem behavior with nonpunitive approaches fall short. In these situations, it is important to contemplate other treatment options based on punishment, including a crisis management protocol to ensure everyone's safety. Like reinforcement, there are two categories of punishment techniques: positive and negative. Regardless of the type of punishment that is selected, it is important to take steps to reduce the likelihood of negative side effects associated with such procedures. This is one of the reasons that these programs will be developed by your supervisor (BCaBA or BCBA). Once the program and its implementation has been explained and perhaps modeled for you, you will need on-going supervision in its implementation. Always include reinforcement procedures for alternative behavior (DRA) as part of the intervention. To do so adheres to our ethical guidelines. It helps to reduce the negative side effects of punishment, and it makes the punishment procedure more effective. Regarding crisis management, it is important to remember you are trying to de-escalate the situation, not teach at that precise moment. Because of the potential for negative side effects and abuse of these procedures, you must always have approval and oversight when implementing them. The oversight must include collecting data on the effects the procedure is having on the problem behavior. It is unethical and non-professional to continue what was thought to be a punitive procedure that is not demonstrating its effectiveness with your client. Moreover, remember neither punishment nor crisis management are teaching strategies: they are reactive strategies geared at preventing and/or reducing problem behavior.

EXERCISES

After you have completed the exercises below, you will want feedback. Your instructor has access (or can obtain access from the publisher) to sample answers for each of the following exercises:

1. Differentiate between timeout and response cost.
2. Describe what you can do to minimize the negative side effects of timeout.
3. Describe how response cost could be implemented in conjunction with a child's allowance.
4. Compare and contrast extinction with response cost.
5. Compare and contrast extinction with planned ignoring.
6. Hector can't read and tends to act out during reading. The laughter he gets from his peers effectively reinforces his stand-up comedy routine and severely interferes with the planned activity. His teacher finally resorts to putting him in timeout in an isolated area of the room with restricted visual access to his peers. This effectively functions to quiet Hector, and the lesson proceeds without him. What impact do you predict this will have on Hector's future behavior during reading? Explain your answer.
7. When using crisis management, you main goal is to _____.
8. Mom wants Kevin to play only in the front yard. Every time he goes in the back yard she spanks him. He now goes in the back yard more than previously. What procedure did mom use on going into the back yard?

ACTIVITIES

1. Describe how you have used, or have seen used, response cost, timeout, negative practice, overcorrection, and corporal punishment. Also, describe how each might have been used more appropriately and effectively, or replaced by a positive behavior intervention. Compare and discuss your experiences with others who know or are learning ABA.

Chapter 13

Comprehensive Behavior Planning

GOALS

1. Describe some rules for developing a professional and collaborative relationship.
2. Describe how one can avoid unprofessional relationships with caregivers.
3. Define treatment integrity and describe how to assess for it.
4. List and describe what you can do to promote treatment integrity.
5. Complete this chapter's exercises/activities or those assigned by your instructor.

*****

Wow—that was a lot of information, and I'm sure you are wondering how to put it all together. In this chapter, we will focus on how to bring all the information presented throughout this book together to ensure you are providing ethical and effective RBT services. This chapter will cover developing professional and collaborative relationships with stakeholders (parents, teachers, caregivers), identifying essential components of behavior plans and preparing for sessions, and reporting other variables besides specified data collection.

Developing Professional and Collaborative Relationships

Use understandable and acceptable language. As you may have observed, behavior analysis utilizes a complex language of its own (such as FBA, DRA, discrimination, operant responding, fading, extinction, etc.). Although it is important for you to know and use this language, there are appropriate contexts and inappropriate contexts in which to use such technological language. *Rule #1: Don't use professional, technical language with those who do not understand it.* We need to know the professional language to be able to attend conferences, read journal articles, and to communicate efficiently with other professionals. However, it is counter to good behavior analytic practice to use such terms with parents, teachers, and caregivers who do not understand them. You should use everyday language when speaking to caregivers as much as possible. Not only will this ensure they understand what you are talking about, but it will also help foster an open line of communication and build rapport with them. These interventions may seem strange and intrusive to them at first, but using a familiar language will make these new interventions less ambiguous and help build a trusting and collaborative relationships with caregivers.

The importance of using comprehensible language is stressed by the BACB: "use language that is fully understandable to the recipient of those services" (2010, p.2). For example, rather than using the term fading, you might say, "fostering independent learning." Instead of scheduling, you might say, "helping the client move toward intrinsic motivation." Rather than extinction, you could say, "appropriate withholding of reinforcement." Rather than response cost, "penalties or fines." For a more complete listing of what you can say in place of the technical language of our field, see Mayer et al. (2014, p. 44).

Use basic communication skills. Another way to ensure an open line of communication is to be an active listener. Just like in every conversation there is a listening and speaking component, it is important to listen to other stakeholders and caregivers. *Rule #2: You should make sure that you schedule at least five minutes per session to listen to the caregivers to get an idea of how things have been going in your absence.* Remember our ultimate goal in behavior analysis is to create behavior change that lasts even when we are not present (i.e., generalization of skills). Besides giving you an idea of what is happening when you are not there, it will also promote a collaborative relationship with the caregivers. In other words, it will help eliminate the "them" vs. "you" separation. Caregivers typically spend the most time with your clients and can provide crucial insight into behaviors, present progress, routines, MOs (antecedents that may influence reinforcing values), etc. In behavior analysis, we model our practice around the client's best interest. Therefore, we are obligated to be active listeners rather than deprive our clients from its proven benefits. Some basic skills with active listening include: not talking or interrupting when they are speaking, rephrasing what they said and then checking for accuracy, and providing empathetic statements (e.g., "I know it is difficult to implement X in public"). It is also important to check for understanding if you have said or explained something to them. This is where it is important to not be judgmental. For example, let's say that Marty's mom just told you about a tantrum at the store. Marty wanted a candy bar, and when she said "No" he threw a huge tantrum. In response to his tantrum, she ended up buying him the candy. It would be easy to think "I taught you how to withhold reinforcement, what were you thinking?" Instead, this information should prompt you to realize you need to go over withholding reinforcement in these types of situations again, rather than blame mom for wrongly implementing the procedure. Before assuming mom's incompetence, consider that this mistake may have been a reflection of your teaching. We can only expect implementers to perform at their skill level, so we must modify the intervention into smaller known tasks (e.g. task analysis) and shape the necessary skills. Nurturing your communication with caregivers will elucidate their present skill levels. Therefore, you can tailor the interventions based off of their strengths. This is a perfect time to empathize with Marty's mom and say, "I know it is hard to withhold reinforcement for problem behavior, especially in public. However, if we want his problem behavior to go away, we *must* not give into him when he throws a tantrum. In this situation, you could have told others looking at you that you are working with an expert and that it is important for everyone to ignore Marty's inappropriate behavior." (Trust me, other moms will understand). In fact, if you ever come across this exact example you could say to the caregiver, "I know a prominent behavior analyst who put her son in timeout in the middle of Disneyland and he started screaming and kicking and she stuck it out even though multiple people were staring at her. Since that occasion, her son has never thrown a tantrum at Disneyland again."

However, there are limits to your help and encouragement. To avoid becoming the family therapist or the mom's best friend, it is important to maintain professional boundaries. You are there to provide services for a specific client, not the caregivers' lives in general. If you start off by drawing this professional line from the beginning, you will be more successful in maintaining it. Crossing the line between friend and therapist diminishes your prestige and authority as a mentor, and it often can cloud your professional judgment. All too often RBTs want to be liked and fit in and end up bending boundaries to do so. You do not have to bend the boundaries to be liked. For example, if the caregiver starts to talk about his or her personal issues not related to your client, politely change the topic back to your client. So, if mom is talking about her problems with dad, ask her a specific question about the client. If these simple re-directions don't work, speak with your supervisor.

As you collaborate with caregivers, try to incorporate the following basic communication skills that have been summarized by Mayer et al. (2014, p. 41):

1. Periodically paraphrase (put into your own words) what the contingency manager is saying to convey your attention and understanding.
2. State any points of confusion and ask for clarification.
3. Summarize the contingency manager's main points within an A-B-C format: "Let's see if I understand what you have shared so far. John tends to hit (B, the behavior) when he is told he can't have something that he want (A, the antecedent or situation) As a result, some-

times he gets what he wants, and at other times he is sent to his room (C, the consequence to the problem behavior)."

4. Make frequent use of "I statements" in gathering information rather than asking too many questions: "I'm a bit confused. I understand that John hits, but I don't have a clear picture of the situations in which this behavior tends to occur. Can you help me gain a clearer picture of that situation?" This format sets a more collaborative tone and prompts a wider range of information than when the person in the role of "expert" seeks information by asking a series of specific questions.

It is important to remember that you are the first line of contact between the stakeholders, caregivers and your BCBA team. Thus, developing this open but professional relationship is paramount to being effective. Medical doctors are judged by their bedside manner, but RBTs are judged on their ability to professionally communicate between caregivers and supervisors.

Essential Components of Behavior Plans and Session Preparation

One thing you may have concluded about implementing behavior analysis is that what you do as a RBT is very specific and based upon a plan (or a general template to guide your actions and responses). Thus, it is advisable to give yourself some time before each session to read over programs so that you implement programming as it was developed by the BCBA.

Treatment integrity refers to the assurance that all program implementers *implement the intervention as planned*. If everyone is conducting the intervention in the same way, there is a greater likelihood that the intervention will be effective. To ensure that you implemented a program as planned, it is important that you understand the program and are trained to competency before implementing the procedures. If you are reviewing programming before initiating services for the day and are confused (even after you have been trained to competency), you should immediately contact your supervisor rather than just winging it. Moreover, if you are in charge of training someone in how to implement a procedure (e.g., parent, aide, nanny), make sure you utilize Behavior Skills Training (instruction, modeling, role playing and feedback). Before having the caregiver implement the program with the client, have them practice and give them feedback until they implement the procedure correctly. Just as we collect data on the client's behavior, we also take data on treatment integrity. Thus, we do not assume someone is implementing the program correctly, but we record which steps were done correctly and incorrectly.

Use checklists. One way to prompt correct implementation and collect treatment integrity data is to create checklists of the programs. Checklists list the various skills the contingency manager (e.g., you, the caretaker, etc.) is to do when implementing the interventions. They serve as effective prompts to remind the contingency manager of what essential skills are to be performed. Basically, they are like a task analysis with each task listed. Break down the intervention into simple steps that are already in the implementer's repertoire, and list each step in the order it should be done. Because it is in our nature to forget things, this minimizes the risk that they will forget a step in the intervention. As each item on the checklist is done, the contingency manger or the assessor places a check next to it. Once completed, these checklists provide good information regarding how well a program is being implemented as planned. If you are required to train caregivers on plans utilizing these checklists, you can record steps as either correct or incorrect. Use these results to give the caregivers feedback on their implementation, because it will specify what steps are being implemented and what needs to be worked on.

Use other prompts. Often, you will find that the contingency managers (caretakers, teachers, etc.) will need to be prompted by you to engage in the intervention skills. Besides your explanations, modeling, and role-playing the intervention for them, they often need additional prompts set up within the natural environment to support the correct implementation of the intervention (treatment integrity). They are not used to doing what you have taught, and there are a lot of other demands on their time. So, it is often helpful if you sit down with the contingency manager and work out a prompting system in addition to checklists (such as, a signal that cues them—"now is the time to complement the client for her behavior"). These cues may include visual prompts strategically displayed in the natural environment (e.g., a posted note), or an auditory prompt that gains the implementer's attention by emitting a sound (e.g., a timer). Finally, do not overlook the client. Clients also can be taught to provide prompts to solicit reinforcement from their contingency managers.

Provide feedback, recognition and praise. A change in the client's behavior is not in itself sufficiently reinforcing to reinforce most contingency managers to continue implementing the intervention with integrity. In addition, they often need praise and recognition. They will need this from you at least twice a week during the first couple of weeks of program implementation, and also from the natural environment. As we pointed out in the chapter on generalization (Chapter 9), you will need to get others in the environment to reinforce the contingency manager's treatment implementation. In the home this could be the spouse or significant other, older siblings of the client's, close friends and/or neighbors, etc. In the classroom this can be a master teacher, administrator, parents, counselor, school psychologist, and others. The point is if the contingency managers use of the intervention is to continue in your absence, it must receive reinforcement from those in the natural environment (you might want to review Chapter 9.) Thus, do not rely just on your prompts and reinforcers to increase program implementation by caretakers, teachers, and others. Prompt others in the natural environment (e.g., home, school, community) to prompt and reinforce program implementation by the contingency managers. As others begin to provide their reinforcers, you need to gradually thin out your use of reinforcers. And, always maintain on-going data collection so that we will know what progress is being made.

Steps to Getting Ready for a Session

1. Read over programs to be implemented.
2. Listen to caregiver and/or staff as to how the client is progressing, and provide positive feedback and support.

3. Gather materials needed to run session.
4. Gather data collection materials.
5. If possible, remove items not necessary for session or that will be a distraction if possible.
6. Initiate contact with client.
7. Start session.
8. Collect data as behavior occurs. (Do not rely on your memory.)

Steps to Complete After Session

1. Put all material away.
2. Update graphs.
3. Write session notes (see below).

These steps can be used regardless of the setting in which you find yourself: that is, regardless of whether you find yourself in a structured setting such as a clinic or classroom or in an unstructured setting such as a park. Ensuring that you are prepared prior to starting a session with a client is extremely important. Think about it as if your shift really starts five minutes before and ends five minutes after the session, because you need to prepare and then close up shop.

Additional Reporting

Besides maintaining behavioral records through valid and reliable data collection and updating graphs, it is also important to keep updated and objective sessions notes. Session notes provide anecdotal descriptions of what happened during a session to illustrate in words what happened that day. They provide a more detailed account than data alone. These notes should include what went well, what did not go so well, any issues that came up during session, any barriers to treatment implementation, or unusual events (e.g., client was sick, a distant family member was visiting). In fact, when reviewing data, it may be important to go back and review session notes if there is an anomaly on the graph. These session notes should include a summary of the programs run, a summary of both appropriate and inappropriate behavior, and specifics regarding implementation of programming. It is important to take the last couple of minutes of the session to record session notes, rather than trying to remember what happened later on after you have seen multiple clients. These notes should be objective in that they describe actual events, and not opinions. Finally, it would be wrong to not remind you that you are a mandatory reporter. If you witness abuse or neglect you *must* report it to state agencies. It is important to have all the details and facts regarding the abuse or neglect so that you can relay the information to the appropriate authorities. Your first step would be to contact your supervisor and then for you and your supervisor to follow reporting procedures.

SUMMARY AND CONCLUSIONS

Knowing behavior analysis is one step in ensuring effective delivery of services. However, it is not enough. To be an effective RBT, you must develop and maintain an appropriate professional relationship that is based upon good communication with the stakeholders and your supervisors. In addition, because the services you provide are so detailed, it is important that you implement services as prescribed by your BCBA. This helps to ensure high levels of treatment integrity that are essential to effective programming and outcomes. Finally, taking objective data on client behavior and detailed notes of events that occur during sessions is imperative to understanding how the services you are delivering are effecting behavior change.

EXERCISES

After you have completed the exercises below, you will want feedback. Your instructor has access (or can obtain access from the publisher) to sample answers for each of the following exercises:

1. Why is using technical language with those who do not understand it non-behavioral?
2. Why is the use of basic communication skills so important when working with those who will be implementing your intervention?
3. Describe why checklists are helpful in prompting those who have frequent contact with the client.
4. Why is it important to provide prompts and feedback?
5. List what you should include to keep updated, objective notes.

ACTIVITIES

1. Practice interchanging professional ABA terms with every day language. Make a game of it and play with a fellow RBT. Write technological terms on one side of a card and pick a card out of the deck. If you can come up with every day language for the term, you get to keep the card. The person with the most cards in the end wins.
2. Follow the steps (role-play) for getting ready and for completing a session.
3. Role-play spending at least five minutes during each session talking to the caregiver(s) regarding how the client has been doing and going over the checklist(s).

References

Baer, D. M., Wolf, M. M., & Risely, T. R. (1968). Some current dimensions of applied behavior analysis. *Journal of Applied Behavior Analysis, 1*, 91–97.

Mayer, G. R., Sulzer-Azaroff, B., & Wallace, M. (2014). *Behavior analysis for lasting change*. 3rd. Edition. Cornwall-on-Hudson, NY: Sloan Publishing.

Sulzer-Azaroff, B. & Associates (2012). *Applying behavior analysis across the autism spectrum: A field guide for practitioners.* 2nd. Edition. Cornwall-on-Hudson: Sloan Publishing.